Don't Ask Why

LEADING WITHOUT LIMITS

Dr. Keith G. Feit

DEDICATION

Don't Ask Why is dedicated to a man who has inspired so many of my leadership beliefs… defying conventional wisdom, challenging the status quo, always questioning… in short, not to conform to what is expected or what is understood to be, but to always be true to who I am in my soul, always digging deeper, wanting more, and defying prescribed limits. Since the day I met him, he has always urged me to make a difference. Thank you, Dr. Ira Bogotch… a professor, a mentor, and most importantly, a dear friend.

CONTENTS

Acknowledgments

Introduction   1

Parable of the Pencil   5

1   Ask Why Not?   7

2   How Can I Help?   17

3   Journey to the Impossible   27

4   The Core Covenant is Sacred   37

5   Conventional Wisdom is Unwise   45

6   Learn to Fail or Fail to Learn   63

7   Empower Your Superheroes   71

8   Establish Your Dream Team   87

9   Get To Know Who's in the Mirror   105

10   Build Bridges, Not Barriers   121

11   Follow the Road Less Traveled   145

12   Evolution or Extinction?   155

13   Feit's Final Limitless Advice   165

Dr. Keith G. Feit

ACKNOWLEDGMENTS

This might seem strange, but I have to thank all those bad, mostly horrendous, pathetic, shameless leaders I have worked with over the years (not all, some were good) for the invaluable learning that was only possible due to their incompetence. I have witnessed the leadership road most travelled - flowing with a robust wave of incompetence and insecurity, lined with an abundance of back-stabbing, deceit, betrayal, and lust for power in a desperate struggle for significance and respect, a path barren of integrity, transparency, honesty, trust, respect, loyalty, and authenticity. Along my leadership expedition, the absolute disgust that has grown within me for that morally corrupt, self-serving leadership that has dominated at the highest levels of business, government, and education, has most assuredly guided my leadership journey toward the road less traveled, where positive impact, making a difference in the lives of others, and leaving the world a better place are the landmarks of which I hold dear.

Introduction

"Leadership is a way of thinking, a way of acting and, most importantly, a way of communicating."

- Simon Sinek

Leadership is not the domain of a few. It is within us all, and with the right mindset, attitude, and preparation, any of us can excel at the art and science of leadership. Leaders fail for many reasons, but the greatest cause of leadership failure has nothing to do with external factors or internal strife, but rather the limitations the leader places on him or herself and the organization… limits that are nothing more than a construct of his or her mind that are born of fear, lack of confidence, or other perceived deficit.

Leadership is an art, with success the result of passion, creativity, and persistence. Artists have the ability to see and to draw what it is that they envision, much the same way that leaders have the ability to dream of a vision and then inspire others to bring that vision to life. To create beautiful art, one must be willing to take risks and accept failure, be their own person and not bother with those who would criticize their work. Doesn't this sound like a leader, who also must accept failure as a step toward success, take risks and try novel approaches, ignoring the whispers of the naysayers and those with hidden personal agendas? The final product of an effective leader, much like the art produced by the world's greatest artists, is nothing less than a beautiful image, risen from overcome struggles and defeated adversity, and born from the leader's spirit and vision.

Leadership is also a science, requiring an exploration of options that involves hypothesizing and experimenting. A leader must be innovative in seeking out and exploiting opportunities, as well as pursuing solutions. Scientists have a propensity for curiosity and are naturally skeptical and inquisitive. Leaders must also be questioning everything, refusing to conform to society and the stale traditions of conventional wisdom and the status quo. One of the most valuable skills a scientist brings to the job is the power of keen observation. While scientists are busy observing specimens, reactions, and other natural phenomenon in the hope of answering real-world questions and solving problems of the natural world, a successful leader must navigate the environment with an eye on potential gaps where there is the prospect of creating opportunities for the organization.

The most compelling reason successful leaders are both artists and scientists is that neither accepts any limits. The power of their passion, skepticism, curiosity, and creativity allow leaders, like artists and scientists, to defy expectations of convention, disregard limits, and create something beautiful. As you will see later, we determine our own limits – those who refuse to accept limits are capable of accomplishing great things; those who allow limits to define their actions and govern their decisions rarely find a way to achieve anything significant.

This book is designed as a guide to help you develop your leadership artistry and master the science of leadership. As with all my work, these words come from my experiences and learning… I do not profess to be omniscient, and I certainly do not have all the answers, but what follows are my beliefs, and the staples of my leadership. I hope not to tell you what to do, but to inspire you to break through your self-determined limits, defy conventional wisdom, challenge the status quo, and exceed expectations on a journey to excellence. Throughout this guide, you will read about my philosophy of leadership, be introduced to some of the strategies I have found powerful and effective, and see quotes from exceptional individuals throughout history that provide support for the lessons contained in these chapters. At the end of each chapter I summarize the lessons contained within, abridged to contain what I believe to be the most important learning from the chapter, and offer some reflection questions that I hope can help you grow.

In the end, I hope you understand the difference between why and why not, and you become a leader that always asks why not.

The Parable of the Pencil

A long time ago a Pencil Maker was preparing to put an important pencil in a box. Before doing so though, he took the pencil aside.

He said, "There are five things you need to know. If you can remember these five things you will become the best pencil you can be."

"First: You will be able to do many great things, but only if you allow yourself to be held in someone else's hand."

"Second: Sharpening is painful, but it is critical if you want to become a better pencil."

"Third: Because you have an eraser, you can correct most mistakes you make, though some may be harder to erase than others."

"Fourth: You may or may not look all that great on the outside, but remember that it's what's inside that's most important; in fact it's your most important part"

"Fifth: Whatever surface you are used on, make sure you leave your mark. No matter how hard, rough or easy, you must continue to write."

Dr. Keith G. Feit

1 Ask Why Not

"Some men see things as they are, and ask why. I dream of things that never were, and ask why not."

— Robert Kennedy

When you approach an opportunity do you think about why you should go for it, or why you shouldn't? This is a very simple but very powerful distinction. On one hand, an individual is training his or her mind to commit only if he or she can find compelling enough reasons to do so. On the other hand, the individual is training him or herself to take chances and go for it, and will only fail to do so if there are compelling reasons against it. Does this make sense?

If an individual asks why, the overwhelming consideration is what can be lost, whereas when an individual asks why not, the prevalent attitude is that there is nothing to lose by taking a chance. It is a focus on what can be gained. Again, simple yet seismic distinction. The choice as to which question you ask yourself when opportunity arises is much more than a simple inquiry - it is a mindset, attitude, life view… why or why not is about how you approach challenges and opportunities!

It has been well documented that one of a leader's main responsibilities is to find, recognize, and exploit opportunities. Let's take it a step further and say that a great leader does not only find existing opportunities the organization can exploit, but he or she actually creates opportunities for the organization. If you, as a leader, are constantly asking why, then it makes sense that your need for compelling reasons to proceed could slow you down enough that the window of opportunity closes, or the gap where an opportunity could have been created ceases to exist. It allows competitors to steal your opportunity and immediately gives away any advantage your organization may have had. If you were to ask why not, the hesitation that causes leaders to miss gaps and opportunities disappears, and the organization has the prospect to exploit an existing opportunity or create one in a recognized gap.

Let's look at an everyday example of the why/why not paradigm… You currently have a job where you make a decent salary, have good benefits, and enjoy your co-workers. The problem is there is no upward mobility; there is no opportunity for you to satisfy your aspirations for a leadership role or to earn a promotion or raise. Another opportunity comes along with a better salary and

ASK WHY…	ASK WHY NOT…
• Why should I take the new job?	• Why shouldn't I take the new job?
• Why should I leave co-workers I like?	• Why shouldn't I be paid more?
• Why leave a job at which I excel for a job I might not be good at?	• Why wouldn't I like the new people?
• Why should I leave for a position that might not work out?	• Why shouldn't I be a leader?
• WHY SHOULD I TAKE A CHANCE?	• Why can't I succeed?
	• WHY SHOULDN'T I TAKE A CHANCE?

benefits, and the position is for the kind of role you were hoping would be available at your current place of employment.

What would you do? Do you take the new job, risking new relationships and possible failure in the new role with the hope of greater success and more happiness, or do you turn it down, sticking with the familiar, continuing to exist in your comfort zone, forfeiting the potential to fulfill your dreams?

If you focus on the negative, how will you ever find your way to the positive?

As you can see from the example… the two questions bring with them a totally different attitude. One takes you further from yes, while the other brings you towards yes. One comes from a negative place while one comes from a positive place. One is anchored in apprehension, while the other is rooted in confidence. One is boosted by hope, while the other is moored in fear. As Abraham Lincoln once said, ***"The probability that we may fail in the struggle ought not to deter us from the support of a cause we believe to be just."*** So too, must we, never shy away from a worthy goal or desired result because there is a possibility that we may not succeed in accomplishing it.

When you make a decision, do you find yourself looking for reasons you should or reasons you shouldn't? Are your thoughts consumed by what can be gained or by what could be lost? Do you generally play it safe or are you a risk-taker? When circumstances change, are you flexible enough to adapt to the new situation? Do you generally find yourself discouraged, apathetic, and/or afraid when approached with new opportunities, or are you hopeful, feeling inspired and empowered to try something new?

Your effectiveness as a leader, in large part, will be an outcome of how you answer these questions. The art of asking why not is a critical component of survival and success in the turbulent environments of the postmodern condition. A leader must be willing to leave the known for the unknown, trade comfort for chaos, and journey beyond the possible into the impossible. You cannot do this if you are looking for reasons to play it safe. You cannot become this kind of dynamic leader if you fear for what could be lost rather than hope for what could be gained.

"Prosperity is not without many fears and distastes; adversity not without many comforts and hopes."
– Francis Bacon

The Power of Why Not

Asking Why	Asking Why Not
Look for reasons not to	Look for reasons to
Focuses on negative outcomes	Focuses on positive outcomes
"Everything to Lose" Attitude	"Nothing to Lose" Attitude
Tendency to play it safe	Tendency to take chances
Promotes inflexible leadership	Promotes flexible leadership and develops resourcefulness
Lessens creativity	Stimulates creativity
Anchored in fear	Anchored in hope
Uninspiring and Discouraging	Inspiring and Empowering
Stymies innovation	Leads to innovation

Your colleagues and subordinates need to trust that you can help them get the job done. When an employee comes to you with an idea, work with him or her to figure out how to get it done. We have a tendency to mold our goals to fit within the resources we have available. In the end, we wind up with a result that is not exactly what we wanted, leading to less satisfaction and perpetuating an organizational culture where settling becomes a norm.

> A leader must be willing to leave the known for the unknown, trade comfort for chaos, and journey beyond the possible into the impossible.

A "why" personality would have a tendency to look for the how first, limiting his or her options, and creating a situation where the best hope is an altered result based on the human, financial, and material resources available. The original question asked becomes, *"What can we do with what we have?"*

A "why not" personality tends to begin with the desired result in mind, concerning himself or herself not with resources available, but rather what needs to be accomplished, then figuring out how to do it. This kind of leader begins with the question, *"How do we get to where we want to be?"*

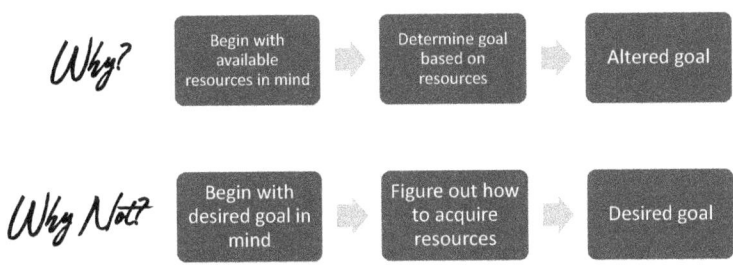

What we should be doing is deciding on our goal, determining what we need to make it happen, and if need be, figuring out how to accumulate the additional resources required to make it become a reality. If we have enough resources -personnel, funds, space – then we simply proceed. If we do not have the resources to achieve our desired result, this is where a leader's creativity comes into play. ***This is finding the way to how.*** It often becomes necessary to think outside of the proverbial box to secure the additional resources. That's OK! Leadership is messy... it involves plenty of mistakes and lessons learned, requires curiosity and creativity, gives rise to plenty of exploration and experimentation, but in the end, it is all about getting the job done! As a leader, your responsibility is to find a way to how, no matter how many twists and turns it takes to get there – not to provide excuses and reasons why your organization can't do something, but to show your colleagues and subordinates, and your bosses if you are in middle management, that you have the ability to always find a way to how, making good ideas become a reality.

Finding a way to how is a critical component of successful leadership, and a leader who has the ability to consistently find the path grants a tremendous advantage to his or her organization.

Asking "why not" and "finding a way to how":

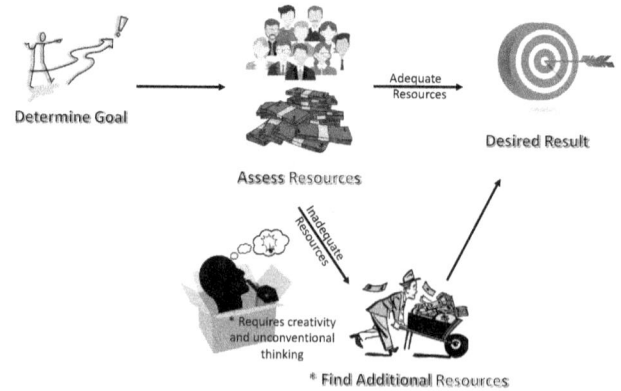

Asking "why not" when new opportunities arise is a way to train yourself to:

- Be more hopeful
- Focus on gain rather than loss
- Make decisions with more confidence
- Develop your creative abilities
- Become more resourceful
- Be more comfortable with taking risks
- Increase your individual and organizational flexibility and adaptability

Asking why not reduces fear and increases hope, stimulating the resourcefulness, creativity, flexibility, and adaptability of a leader.

Why or Why Not?

For each item below, read the statements in Column A and Column B that would complete the statement. Determine which of those two choices best describes you and place the letter of the column in the column labeled "Your Choice."

COLUMN A	YOUR CHOICE	COLUMN B
1. When I go into a new venture…		
I worry about what I am leaving behind.		*I think about the new possibilities.*
2. When a new opportunity presents itself…		
I tend to find reasons I shouldn't go for it.		*I tend to find reasons I should go for it.*
3. I determine my available resources…		
Before I figure out what I want to accomplish.		*After I figure out what I want to accomplish.*
4. I tend to focus on…		
The things that are holding me back from accomplishing my goal.		*The things I can do to accomplish my goal.*
5. If I think something I want to do is unrealistic or unattainable…		
I create a more realistic goal.		*I think of different ways I can achieve the goal.*

For each "B" you chose, give yourself 1 point. For each "A" you choose, give yourself 0 points.

ITEM	YOUR CHOICE	SCORE (1 or 0)	RESULT
1			If you scored 3, 4, or 5, you are more of a "Why Not" leader.
2			
3			
4			If you scored 0, 1, or 2, you are more of a "Why" leader.
5			
TOTAL	**************		

Why Ask Why Not?

Do not limit yourself by trying to figure out what you can do with the resources you have...

| Ask why? | Determine resource limits before deciding what to do? | Adjust goals to be able to accomplish within limits | Altered Result |

Figure out what you want to do and then figure out how to get the resources you need to make it work!

| Ask why not? | Determine what you want to do, regardless of resource limitations? | Figure out how to overcome limits to accomplish goals | Desired Result |

2 How Can I Help?

"I hold that while man exists, it is his duty to improve not only his own condition, but to assist in ameliorating mankind."

— Abraham Lincoln

U.S. Vice President Mike Pence is quoted as saying, "I believe in servant leadership, and the servant always asks, 'Where am I needed most?'" Merriam Webster defines a servant as "one who serves," especially "one that performs duties about the person or home of a master or personal employer." This definition does not paint a flattering picture of one who serves, making it sound as though all the power is in the hands of the master. A traditional servant would agree, living and working at the behest of his or her master. Throughout history, we have seen too many examples of cruel masters – people who enslaved those they considered inferior races, and individuals who exploited young boys and girls in the form of child labor, among others – who have promulgated the thought of servant as powerless and often unworthy of human dignity, whose only purpose is to ensure the master is satisfied.

"I don't know what your destiny will be, but one thing I do know – the only ones among you who will be really happy are those who have sought and found how to serve." – Albert Schweitzer

This could not be further from the truth in the realm of leadership. While a servant is powerless, a servant leader has all the power. By serving those who follow, a leader develops trust and respect with his or her followers, earning their loyalty and gaining commitment in pursuing the vision and mission of the organization. Trust, respect, loyalty, commitment... these are the sources of power a leader effectively utilizes to align members in the same direction, providing them ownership in the outcomes of the organization and empowering them to help propel the organization forward. Leading from the bottom up empowers followers, leading to commitment. Leading from the top down controls followers, gaining compliance.

> Trust, respect, loyalty, commitment... these are the sources of power a leader effectively utilizes to align members in the same direction, providing them ownership in the outcomes of the organization and empowering them to help propel the organization forward.

Robert Greenleaf, the seminal researcher studying servant leadership, suggests that a servant leader has a true desire to serve, and that is his or her ultimate purpose. The Greenleaf Center for

Servant Leadership defines servant leadership as, "a philosophy and set of practices that enriches the lives of individuals, builds better organizations, and ultimately creates a more just and caring world."

While I believe in servant leadership, and agree that a leader's primary role is to serve those within the organization, this chapter is not simply about servant leadership...

> Leading from the bottom up empowers followers, leading to commitment. Leading from the top down controls followers, gaining compliance.

Regardless of the type of leader you are, it is critical for you to earn the support of your subordinates. There are many ways to do this – earning commitment through building relationships, gaining compliance through intimidation, acquiring cooperation through transactions – and each of these result in a different level of outcomes. Commitment is by far the most powerful form of employee pledge toward the organization, and to gain commitment a leader must find a way to show the employee that what is best for the organization is also what is best for the individual. ***By demonstrating a commitment to the individual, the leader can gain commitment from the individual.***

"No one is useless in this world who lightens the burden of another." – Charles Dickens

How does a leader show this commitment to the individual and gain commitment to the organization? The answer is to ask a question – a specific question that says everything that needs to be said:

How Can I Help?

As a leader, your job is to ensure that your followers have everything they need to be successful. The best thing you can do is to always be there to help in any way possible, offer any assistance needed, and support in every way, constantly making it clear that leader and follower are on the same team and chasing the same goal. The choice is always there to be a boss - commanding, demanding, reprimanding – or to be a leader – supporting, assisting, and accompanying – on the journey to either success or failure.

A boss drives the effort from a position of power, involved in the struggles only as far as directing efforts. A leader, however, immerses him or herself into the action, equally living the struggle, driving the effort from the front lines. What does this have to do with the "ask why not" paradigm? It's simple - an individual far removed from the battle typically has an ask why philosophy, always needing a reason to provide assistance; a leader at the front lines asks why not, needing a reason not to provide assistance, without which he or she will always err in favor of supporting followers. Thus, "asking why not" and "how can I help" are directly correlated, with an individual that asks why not consistently more likely to seek out ways to assist those who share a common goal.

"The best way to find yourself is to lose yourself in service to others." – Mahatma Gandhi

Leaders are different, and not all are willing to lower themselves to the level of their followers, or dirty their hands completing the tasks they ordered to be accomplished. Not all believe in seeking ways that they can assist those under their command. This reminds me of the story of the man and the soldiers:

Sometime, close to a battlefield over 200 years ago, a man in civilian clothes rode past a small group of exhausted battle-weary soldiers digging an obviously important defensive position. The section leader, making no effort to help, was shouting orders, threatening punishment if the work was not completed within the hour.

"Why are you are not helping?" asked the stranger on horseback.

"I am in charge. The men do as I tell them," said the section leader, adding, "Help them yourself if you feel strongly about it."

To the section leader's surprise, the stranger dismounted and helped the men until the job was finished.

Before leaving, the stranger congratulated the men for their work, and approached the puzzled section leader.

"You should notify top command next time your rank prevents you from supporting your men - and I will provide a more permanent solution," said the stranger.

Up close, the section leader now recognized General Washington, and also the lesson he'd just been taught.

Asking "How can I help?" accomplishes the following:

- Builds trust
- Empowers followers
- Promotes collaboration
- Gains commitment
- Engenders loyalty

The "How Can I Help?" Paradigm:

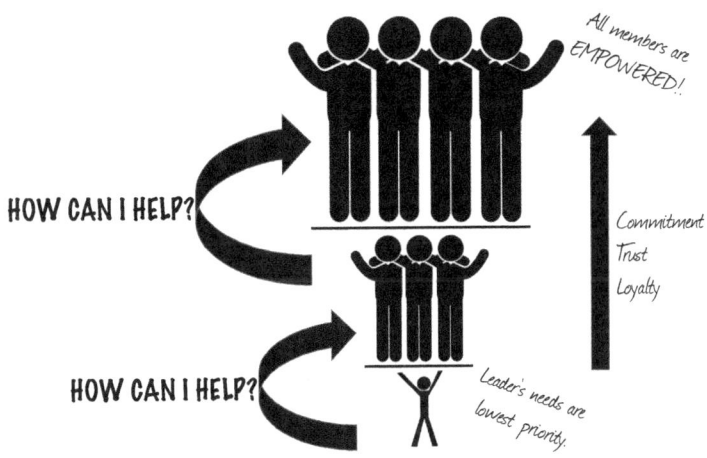

What does this graphic show us? First, and foremost, it displays the primary principle behind this philosophy – the leader serves those subordinate to him/her. This occurs by asking "How Can I Help" to those at the next level – top executives asking middle management, middle management asking team supervisors, team supervisors asking team members, etc. It is clearly a bottom up approach to leadership, that if implemented with fidelity creates an organization where all members are leaders and feel valued.

Secondly, we see the difference in size as one moves from one level to the next. Why? Because the needs of the employees are far more important than the personal needs of the leader. A leader gains the greatest commitment from employees by ensuring that their needs are met. Employees who are satisfied promote high morale in the workplace, typically leading to more commitment and better productivity.

Thirdly, we see that by asking how he or she can help, a leader empowers members of the organization, not only giving them the tools to complete tasks and make decisions, but also giving them the motivation and desire to do so. They are presented largest in size in the graphic because they are most critical to organizational success.

Finally, we clearly see the upward traveling arrow, symbolizing that through this paradigm, greater empowerment occurs as we move from one level to the next, promoting the development of stronger interpersonal relationships with the increase in trust, loyalty, and commitment to the cause.

By asking, "How can I help?" a leader opens the door to empowerment by making it clear that the needs of the individual are important and the leader is there to support in any and all endeavors to help an employee complete their task toward organizational success. It is a total team effort from start to finish. This simple question advances trust and increases the individual's comfort zone, ensuring each individual that they have a companion on their journey, rather than a bully. Albert Einstein once said, *"The high destiny of the individual is to serve rather than rule."* A leader is judged not on the ability to force others to do what he or she commands, but on the ability to inspire others to do more than they thought they could. Rather than drive members of an organization toward a chosen destination like a herd of sheep, a leader guides them in the same direction toward the organizational goal with autonomy, empowerment, and support.

> A leader is judged not on the ability to force others to do what he or she commands, but on the ability to inspire others to do more than they thought they could.

A "How can I help" philosophy empowers a leader and followers while promoting strong interpersonal relationships and a supportive culture.

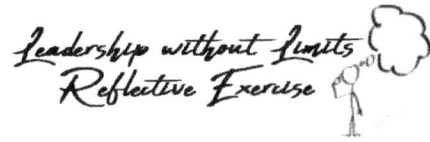

DO I HAVE A HELP MINDSET?

Directions: Circle the number that best represents how you feel about each of the items below.

1. If an employee wants to build a new product she believes will improve profits but we do not have the resources to begin production, I have to deny the request.

1	2	3	4	5
Strongly Disagree		*Neutral*		*Strongly Agree*

2. If one of my subordinates is consistently struggling to accomplish the tasks I have assigned without assistance, my initial thought is that I have hired the wrong person.

1	2	3	4	5
Strongly Disagree		*Neutral*		*Strongly Agree*

3. I am not empowering my employees if I offer to help.

1	2	3	4	5
Strongly Disagree		*Neutral*		*Strongly Agree*

4. As a leader, it is my responsibility to ensure my employees can complete their tasks with little to no assistance.

1	2	3	4	5
Strongly Disagree		*Neutral*		*Strongly Agree*

5. I expect my supervisors to focus more on my directives than the needs of their subordinates.

1	2	3	4	5
Strongly Disagree		*Neutral*		*Strongly Agree*

6. Trust, respect, and loyalty are hindered when a leader helps a subordinate accomplish a task.

1	2	3	4	5
Strongly Disagree		*Neutral*		*Strongly Agree*

Scoring the "Do I Help?" Questionnaire:

Directions: Add up the score you selected for each item in the questionnaire.

ITEM #	SCORE
1	
2	
3	
4	
5	
6	
TOTAL	

If you scored below 12, you have a help mindset.

If you scored 13-23, you have a mindset that could become a help mindset with work.

If you scored over 24, you do not have a help mindset.

Reflection Question:

What is your first reaction when someone comes to you for assistance? Do you ask, "How can I help?," and mean it?

3 Journey to the Impossible

"It always seems impossible until it is done."

— Nelson Mandela

Who determines what is possible? Why do so many things that once seemed impossible all of a sudden join the realm of the possible? If we think seriously about it, the impossible is often a state of mind; it is frequently something that is so difficult that we train our minds that it cannot be done.

There are certain things we will never be able to physically do. That is not what journeying to the impossible is about. When we speak of journeying to the impossible, we are actually speaking about the possibilities in our minds. We are speaking of the limitations we place on ourselves, our colleagues, and our organizations. Why does peace in the Middle East seem impossible?

Is it because we, as humans, do not have the ability to live with people of other religions, races, and ethnicities in harmony? Can two groups of people not occupy the same land while maintaining the prideful celebrations of their different cultures? If we think about it, all the differences in the world are not keeping the world from such peace, but it is the limitations in the minds, hearts, and souls of those involved in the process that has constructed the barrier to peaceful coexistence.

What is the impossible?

"There is nothing impossible to him who will try."
- Alexander the Great

The impossible is a construct of the human mind. We determine that what we find extremely difficult, what we see as unrealistic, what we believe to be unfeasible… these things are impossible. The impossible is nothing more than a set of limits that we place on ourselves that prevents our minds from believing we can achieve the outcome. As famous author, philanthropist, and life coach, Tony Robbins, says, ***"What we can or cannot do, what we consider possible or impossible, is rarely a function of our true capability. It is more likely a function of our beliefs about who we are."***

Why?

I believe it is because we are so afraid of failure that we construct this alternate reality of the impossible in order to prevent us from attempting the unknown and risking disappointment. To attempt to accomplish something that has not been done before, something that may be dangerous, difficult, and seemingly not a fit for our individual talents, skills, and attributes is a high risk endeavor... the chance of failure is great, the possibility of tremendous disappointment is pronounced, and the potential to seem inadequate, weak, or incompetent to others is undeniable.

The impossible, therefore, is but a figment of our individual imagination, or lack thereof. When we construct these artificial, self-imposed limitations, we are restricting ourselves to a very small range of possibilities, with most truly worthy opportunities beyond the reach of our restrained minds. The fear of failure is extremely powerful, and when we allow that fear to control our thoughts, hopes, and aspirations, we create the realm of the impossible, constructing an almost impenetrable barrier to the unknown.

> The impossible is nothing more than a set of limits that we place on ourselves, preventing our minds from believing we can achieve the outcome.

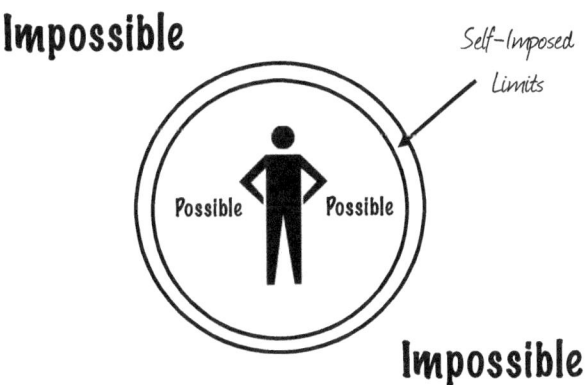

It is important to remember that fear only has power over us if we allow it to. As President Franklin Roosevelt famously said during the Great Depression, ***The only thing we have to fear, is***

fear, itself." Fear is a constant companion, always whispering in your ear telling you that you can't do something or something bad is going to happen. As I wrote in *Be A Bean*, ignore the whispers of others. This goes for the whispers of fear, as well. Learn from the lesson offered in the following Buddhist parable:

> *Once there was a young warrior. Her teacher told her that she had to do battle with fear. She didn't want to do that. It seemed too aggressive; it was scary; it seemed unfriendly. But the teacher said she had to do it and gave her the instructions for the battle.*
>
> *The day arrived. The student warrior stood on one side, and fear stood on the other. The warrior was feeling very small, and fear was looking big and wrathful. They both had their weapons. The young warrior roused herself and went toward fear, prostrated three times, and asked, "May I have permission to go into battle with you?" Fear said, "Thank you for showing me so much respect that you ask permission."*
>
> *Then the young warrior said, "How can I defeat you?" Fear replied, "My weapons are that I talk fast, and I get very close to your face. Then you get completely unnerved, and you do whatever I say. If you don't do what I tell you, I have no power. You can listen to me, and you can have respect for me. You can even be convinced by me. But if you don't do what I say, I have no power." In that way, the student warrior learned how to defeat fear.*

Think about where you are now… Have you accomplished all of which you are capable? Have you made the biggest difference you can possibly make? Have you had the greatest positive impact you could have? If not, why not? How much have you limited yourself by saying, "I can't do that," "It's not worth it," "One person can't make a difference," "Nothing will change," "Other people won't agree with me." There are many more questions we ask ourselves that construct that wall of limitations that surrounds us and protects us from the unknown we construct as the impossible. How much of that barrier, those limits, are constructed out of fear? Now, think about some of those who found a way to defeat fear and refused to set limits –

Walt Disney, whose company is now the largest entertainment company in the world and possibly the most universally recognized international brand, was a man who was denied a job at a newspaper because he "lacked creativity." The man who created the most recognized and beloved animated characters in history, and developed the "happiest place on Earth," Walt Disney World, visited by an average of 52 million people each year and a dream trip for children of all ages, was told he was incapable of creative thought. He challenged that assessment, refused to set personal limits, and journeyed to his impossible. This could be why he was quoted as saying, *"It's kind of fun to do the impossible."*

Historically, no individual has ever achieved greater military success at a younger age than Alexander the Great, who conquered most of the known world between 336 and 323 BCE. He assumed the throne from his father, Philip of Macedon, an extremely successful king in his own right, and at the young age of 20 refused to be restrained by the limits of previous kings or those his advisors would try to place on him. Although his life was cut short by illness, Alexander stretched his empire from Greece to India, conquering the ancient powers of the Persian and Egyptian empires, never once losing a battle. His achievement was so incredible that none other than Julius Caesar, the great Roman general and dictator who led the greatest empire ever known to man, cried at a statue of Alexander and declared in envy, *Do you think I have not just cause to weep, when I consider that Alexander at my age had conquered so many nations, and I have all this time done nothing that is memorable?"*

The king of innovation, the late Apple Founder and CEO, Steve Jobs, was known to challenge limits. In fact, when Jobs was told he couldn't do something, that is exactly what he did. When the rest of the world limited the use of computers, Jobs pushed the limits by bringing computers to the masses. He revolutionized cell phones, further bringing portable processing power to our fingertips with the introduction of the iPhone. The animated film industry was revolutionized by his introduction of Pixar. He was so skilled at pushing the boundaries of human ingenuity that it was often said he had a reality distortion field that propelled his people into the impossible. Those who refuse to accept limits and dare to travel to the impossible are those who improve lives, shape communities, advance society, and change the world… or as Steve Jobs calls them, the crazy ones,

> *"Here's to the crazy ones, the misfits, the rebels, the troublemakers, the round pegs in the square holes… the ones who see things differently — they're not fond of rules… You can quote them, disagree with them, glorify or vilify them, but the only thing you can't do is ignore them because they change things… they push the human race*

forward, and while some may see them as the crazy ones, we see genius, because the ones who are crazy enough to think that they can change the world, are the ones who do."

These men succeeded where others have failed because they do not see an impossible. They see a universe of possibilities. As we said earlier, the impossible is created by the limits we place on ourselves - things we are afraid to do, things we think we cannot do – whatever the reason, it all begins in our mind. Once our mind tells our heart we can't do it, we can't. Confucius wrote, **"Those who think they can and those who think they can't are both usually right."** To succeed in journeying to the impossible, we must clear our minds of the limits we have created, much as the Zen Master advises in the parable below,

Once, a professor went to a Zen Master. He asked him to explain the meaning of Zen. The Master quietly poured a cup of tea. The cup was full but he continued to pour. The professor could not stand this any longer, so he questioned the Master impatiently, "Why do you keep pouring when the cup is full?" "I want to point out to you," the Master said, "that you are similarly attempting to understand Zen while your mind is full. First, empty your mind of preconceptions before you attempt to understand Zen."

In the same way, you must empty your mind of limits before we attempt to achieve something. Your mind controls the key to your journeys, it controls your limits, your beliefs, and the perception of the environment in which you find yourself. American writer, Mark Caine, wrote, **"The first step toward success is taken when you refuse to be a captive of the environment in which you first find** *yourself.*" Do not become a captive stranded in the realm of the possible that your self-imposed limits have constructed - step beyond that environment, reach beyond your supposed limits, leave your comfort zone, and dare to journey to the impossible. Remember, things are only impossible because they have never been done before. You have the power to make the impossible a reality by fighting through fear and venturing into the unknown.

A philosophy I always try to remember, and one that I hope continues to guide my leadership and life is simple, yet powerful, and can make a world of difference in your leadership if you subscribe to it…

The only way to discover the limits of the possible is to go beyond them into the impossible.

*Leadership without Limits
Reflective Exercise*

JOURNEYING TO THE IMPOSSIBLE

1. Think about your life.

    a. What personal limits have you placed on yourself?

    b. What professional limits are keeping you from your goals?

2. What opportunities are trapped in your impossible?

3. How can you challenge your limits and journey to your impossible?

4 The Core Covenant is Sacred

"There are only two options regarding the commitment to a Core Covenant. You are either IN or you're OUT. There's no such thing as life in-between."

— *Pat Riley*

Every team, organization, or civilization commits to a core set of values and beliefs. Whether written, verbal, or simply by repeated action, these values and beliefs are what bind the group together, motivating and inspiring each other to be accountable to one another, to be responsible for their obligations, and to guide their actions in an effort to achieve a common goal. President Abraham Lincoln famously said, ***"A house divided against itself cannot stand."*** This is the importance of the core covenant… Why?

The core covenant is the promise or promises a leader makes to his or her followers and the organization, and the promises the followers make to the leader, the organization, and to each other. The core covenant is the foundation of the culture, providing the blueprint for the common language, values, and beliefs to be shared in pursuit of the organization's vision and mission. It is a powerful tool empowering the leader by helping to ensure that all oars row in the same direction.

> The core covenant is the foundation of the culture, providing the blueprint for the common language, values, and beliefs to be shared in pursuit of the organization's vision and mission.

The covenant is not something that can be forced on members of the organization. While the leader can create an atmosphere where members commit to promises aligned with those of the leader, the covenant must be developed collaboratively, with leader and follower both contributing to the determination of the most important promises to be made by all stakeholders.

General Stanley Chrystal, retired 4-star U.S. Army General, head of the Joint Special Operations Command and Commander of U.S. forces in Afghanistan, said political campaigns *"offer Americans an opportunity to adjust direction, reaffirm values, and recommit to the covenant that binds them together."* The greatest campaign in the life of an organization is that which attempts to fulfill its mission and bring its vision to fruition. As such, the establishment of the vision and mission is the time for members of the organization to align with the direction of the organization, reassert their core values, and commit their individual promises to fulfillment of the core covenant. Once bonded by commitment to the covenant, it is critical that leaders ensure all members are adhering to their pledges and fulfilling the promises of the core covenant.

"*A house divided against itself cannot stand.*"
– Abraham Lincoln

Establishing a Core Covenant

Steps to Establishing a Core Covenant

1. Develop Shared Vision and Mission

2. Determine Core Values and Shared Beliefs

3. Design Plan for Fulfilling Mission and Realizing Vision

4. Communicate Individual Promises

Successful leadership starts and ends with buy-in from followers. If members of the organization are aligned with the vision and mission of the organization, there becomes a draft wind at the leader's sail. Without buy-in, there is tremendous headwind. The easiest way to ensure buy-in is to involve the rank and file in the development of a shared vision and mission for the organization. If a vision and mission already exist, use your authority as leader to revise the vision and mission to include input from those currently serving in the organization, as long as those revisions are in line with the original purposes. Just make sure all members have an opportunity to provide input.

Once establishing the shared vision and mission of the organization, or coming to a strong understanding of the existing vision and mission, it becomes necessary to determine the core values and shared beliefs of the organization. What do we believe? How do we do things? What values do we hold dear? Basically, this is the establishment of the desired culture.

Based upon the vision, mission, values, and shared beliefs, how can we make our vision a reality? How can we fulfill our mission? This stage is where the blueprint for actualization is laid out. How do we get where we want to go? What things do we need to do to ensure we fulfill our purpose in this organization? This is when the membership and leadership, together, determine the path forward and the promises each member must make in order to get to the "promised land."

The leader first needs to determine the most important promises he or she can make to the other stakeholders. It is impossible to promise everything, so the best thing to do is to focus on a few critical aspects in which you can help the organization fulfill its mission, and your followers to reach their potential. I suggest three promises is the ideal commitment the leader can make to the other members of the organization that you will undertake in an effort to facilitate fulfillment of the vision.

> It is impossible to promise everything, so the best thing to do is to focus on a few critical aspects in which you can help the organization fulfill its mission, and your followers to reach their potential.

Once the leader establishes his/her commitment to the covenant, he or she can then request commitments from each group of stakeholders. For example, in a school, the principal and administrators establish their promises in the covenant, followed by the faculty and staff, the students, and the parents. All groups of stakeholders MUST commit to the covenant for it to be an effective alignment tool.

> A positive core covenant can only be established in an atmosphere of mutual trust and respect.

A positive core covenant can only be established in an atmosphere of mutual trust and respect. The stronger the interpersonal and professional relationships that have been nurtured throughout the organizational culture, the easier it is to establish a positive covenant. The establishment of this atmosphere is one of the most critical requirements of an effective leader.

Elements of a Positive Core Covenant

All core covenants are going to be different, depending on the geography, industry, organization, and individuals that compose the organization. That being said, there are a few universal components of a positive core covenant.

First and foremost, the promises must be REAL. They must be made from the heart and they must be true to the convictions of the individual making them. Insincere promises, those not from the heart, will not be kept and will lead to a false covenant. Such a false covenant has the potential to contaminate the organizational culture with deleterious personal agendas and hidden animosities, fostering a weakening of interpersonal relationships. The purpose of a covenant, to guide all members in the same direction, is then impossible, as the personal agendas and hidden objectives of a false covenant drive members in various directions, many being way off course of the intended path of the organization.

Secondly, there must be transparency in any and all words and actions within an organization, especially when making the promises that will form the core covenant. There is no room for hidden agendas when entering into the organization's critical individual promises. Individual members must be honest with themselves and their peers, promising only those things that they believe in their heart are important, feasible, and aligned toward the vision of the organization.

Finally, the various promises entered into within the core covenant must be symbiotic with each other. Each individual promise must fit together so that when each piece of the covenant puzzle is put together, a beautiful vision is the final outcome. Not only does each promise have to be aligned with the vision, but each promise must be supportive of one another, so that none negate the positive impact of any others.

The Core Covenant is the sacred blueprint for organizational culture, and requires transparent and honest commitment from all members.

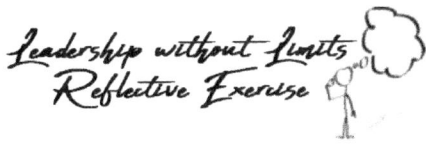

ESTABLISHING THE CORE COVENANT

1. What are the vision and mission of your organization?

2. What can you promise your stakeholders that you will always do to ensure fulfillment of the mission and realization of the vision?

3. What promises would you like from your organizational members that they can make in an effort to fulfill the mission and realize the vision?

4. How can you bring the reality of the Core Covenant to fruition in your organization?

Below is an example of a Core Covenant worksheet for a school environment.

Directions: Choose three promises you pledge to fulfill as the leader of your organization. Then choose three promises you wish for each set of stakeholders to fulfill as members of your educational community.

Our Covenant

This is my covenant with my faculty, staff, students, and parents. I will make a promise to fulfill my core covenant to the best of my ability and will ask the other members of my community to do the same.

My core covenant:

1.

2.

3.

Teachers covenant:

1.

2.

3.

Students covenant:

1.

2.

3.

Parents covenant:

1.

2.

3.

5 Conventional Wisdom is Unwise

"Swim upstream. Go the other way. Ignore the conventional wisdom."

- Sam Walton

The world's largest retailer, WalMart, was built by a man (Sam Walton) who believed that conventional wisdom was something that not only warranted little adherence, but should actually be ignored. He suggested purposely doing the opposite of what was expected. Apple, the world's most profitable public company, was built much in the same way by founder Steve Jobs, whose innovations have changed the way we interact with the digital world and communicate with our friends, and has actually fostered a world of easily accessed international interconnectivity.

Jobs is quoted as saying,

> *"Your time is limited, so don't waste it living someone else's life. Don't be trapped by dogma - which is living with the results of other people's thinking. Don't let the noise of others' opinions drown out your own inner voice. And most important, have the courage to follow your heart and intuition."*

In *Be A Bean*, we put it slightly different but with the same central message. One of the Beanitudes, or core platitudes, is to *"listen to the shout of your heart, not the whispers in your ears."* In other words, ignore the whispers of others, with their personal schemes and hidden agendas, and those who would lead you astray. Where we say "shout of your heart," Jobs says "your inner voice." What Jobs calls, "the noise of others' opinions" is what we refer to as "whispers in your ears."

If you think like everyone else, how will anything ever change?

Dogma, as Steve Jobs calls it, will lead to stagnation, an environment void of innovation. After all, if you think like everyone else, how can anything ever change? If you want to be a true leader, then you wish to see change – progress, growth, development – whatever you wish to call it. We do not get progress from thinking like everyone else, from confining ourselves to the conventional wisdom of the day. We achieve progress by thinking differently,

> We achieve progress by thinking differently, by never being satisfied with where we are or what we have, but always trying to think bigger, do better, and be more.

by never being satisfied with where we are or what we have, but always trying to think bigger, do better, and be more. After all, **we should always focus not on what we are, but what we can become**.

 *"Discontent is the first necessity of progress."*
– Thomas Edison

Although leaders and managers do many of the same things, and they share certain attributes, there is a huge difference between the two. It is a leader who provides the direction while a manager keeps the organization on course. While a manager maintains an orderly process with rigid procedures and transactional methods, a leader flirts with chaos, guiding the organization toward a vision that often involves organizational transformation. Managers can think conventionally, maintaining the processes that have led to the current state, but leaders MUST think differently. Leaders must think outside of the proverbial box, challenge conventional wisdom, and disrupt the status quo for positive change to occur. That positive change is called progress.

> Leaders must think outside of the proverbial box, challenge conventional wisdom, and disrupt the status quo for positive change to occur.

Let's not act, however, as though conventional wisdom is always wrong. The way we behave in certain situations and around certain people, certain ways of thinking that keep us safe, and many of the things we learn as we grow up are all part of conventional wisdom that we are wise to follow. However, when talking about leadership, we are talking about thinking differently to achieve progress. It means being proactive when others are reactive. It means creativity and ingenuity where others settle for the unimaginative. It means being unorthodox when others conform to convention. It means learning to do things differently as circumstances change, as the ladies in the following parable teach us:

A little girl was watching her mother prepare a fish for dinner. Her mother cut the head and tail off the fish and then placed it into a baking pan. The little girl asked her mother why she cut the head and tail off the fish.

Her mother thought for a while and then said, "I've always done it that way - that's how grandma did it."

Not satisfied with the answer, the little girl went to visit her grandma to find out why she cut the head and tail off the fish before baking it.

Grandma thought for a while and replied, "I don't know. My mother always did it that way."

So the little girl and the grandma went to visit great grandma to ask if she knew the answer.

Great grandma thought for a while and said, "Because my baking pan was too small to fit the whole fish."

Simply doing things a certain way because that is how they have always been done is not a recipe for growth and progress, it's a recipe for stagnation. Just as larger pans could have fit whole fish and required less work for the women, thinking differently could lead to more effective and efficient processes that lead to better outcomes. Again, conventional wisdom, in this case the way things have always been done, is not always wise.

Let's have a little vocabulary lesson and look at the synonyms, antonyms, and other words related to conventional:

Word	Definition	Synonyms/Related Words	Antonyms
Conventional	Accepted, used, or practiced by most people	Usual, average, common, ordinary	Unusual, uncommon, exceptional, extraordinary
	based on customs usually handed down from a previous generation	Traditional, established, usual, common, old-time, old-world	Original, Nonconformist, unprecedented, progressive, revolutionary

Source: Merriam-Webster Dictionary

As a leader, do you wish to be seen as the usual - ordinary, average, common, and old-world (belonging to a tradition whose time has passed) - or would you prefer to be seen as an original - uncommon, exceptional, extraordinary, and progressive, belonging not to the past, but to the future? Is it more important for you to please those stuck in the ways of the past and follow tradition to a future of similar results or to ride a revolutionary zest for progress to a brighter future? Are you content being like everyone else or do you wish to establish yourself as your own person, and leave a legacy of great accomplishment and a better world?

Being content breeds conformity. Conformity begets ordinary. Ordinary yields average results. Average results lead to stagnancy.

Discontent breeds nonconformity. Nonconformity begets extraordinary. Extraordinary yields exceptional results. Exceptional results lead to progress.

Conventional wisdom leads to predictable results; results we have already seen. Unorthodox thinking leads to unknown results, results we have not seen but hold the potential for far greater achievement. While unorthodox thinking holds a greater potential for failure, there is also greater potential for a higher yield. Nonconformity can open a whole new world…

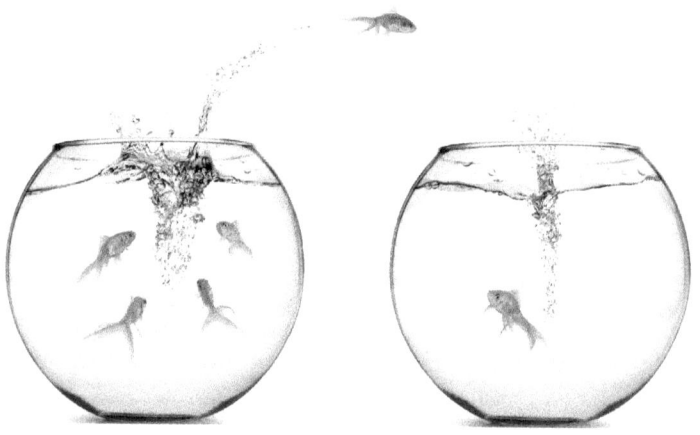

Training for Nonconformity

The easiest thing in the world is to be like everyone else. If you don't stand out, you are safe… the herd mentality. That is all well and good if your ultimate goal is simply to survive, to do nothing more than exist with as little effort as possible. If your goal is to play it safe and depart this world with not even a footprint of you having been a part of it, then join the herd.

If, however, your desire is to leave your mark on society, to have a positive impact and make a difference while you are here, then you must break away from the herd. You must be willing to stand out on a ledge, alone and vulnerable, sometimes challenging all that is known and cherished. As author Marty Rubin says, *"Freedom began on the day the first sheep wandered away from the herd."*

To lead is to put yourself in danger, to put yourself out front, to put yourself in the loneliest position. Leadership is not a safe proposition… upon accepting the role of leader, an individual has invited a bulls eye on his or her back. The leader instantly becomes the embodiment of every problem, setback, and failure. The leader becomes a magnet for the anger, unhappiness, and dissatisfaction of his or her followers. The leader must deal with both internal and external threats, and often must stand alone in the face of grave opposition. But if you choose to be a leader…

You can make a difference. You can provide a vision for a better future, and offer an alignment to guide the organization to that future. You can alter minds and hearts and bring people together to achieve something amazing!

If this is what you want to do, to leave much more than a mere footprint on your organization, your community, your nation, or perhaps even the world, then you need to learn to be your own person. You need to learn to stand up to conventional wisdom, to challenge the status quo, and to think and act differently. In short, you need to train yourself in nonconformity.

> *"The worst curse to befall anyone is stagnation, a banal existence, the quiet desperation that comes out of a need for conformity."* – Deepak Chopra

The Blueprint for Nonconformity

1. Think Differently
2. Question Everything
3. Feed Your Discontent

Thinking Differently

Albert Einstein said, ***"We cannot solve our problems with the same thinking we used when we created them."*** Thinking differently is a key to effective leadership and a must for a leader who wants to challenge the status quo and implement change. We cannot achieve progress if we do not think differently than the thought processes that have brought us to where we currently are.

"Conformity is that jailer of freedom and the enemy of growth."
- John F. Kennedy

Thinking differently, as I was taught by Dr. John Pisapia, is perhaps the most important ability of a leader. Thinking differently means not thinking like others, not thinking conventionally... it means thinking outside the box, thinking unorthodoxly, and sometimes thinking crazy! The ability to think differently not only gives the leader a tremendous advantage over those who can only think conventionally, but it also means that there is always another way – if one can think differently, then he or she can quite possibly find a way out of a seemingly impossible situation. This brings to mind a story I came across one day on wealthygorilla.com (paraphrased):

In a small Italian town, hundreds of years ago, a small business owner owed a large sum of money to a loan-shark, who was very old and unattractive and it just so happened that he fancied the business owner's daughter.

He decided to offer the businessman a deal that would completely wipe out the debt he owed him, with just one catch - he would only wipe out the debt if he could marry the businessman's daughter.

Needless to say, this proposal was met with a look of disgust, so the loan-shark altered the deal.

The loan-shark said that he would place two pebbles into a bag, one white and one black.

The daughter would reach into the bag and pick out a pebble. If it was black, the debt would be wiped out and the loan-shark would marry the daughter. If it was white, the debt would still be wiped out, but the daughter wouldn't have to marry the loan-shark.

Standing on a pebble-strewn path in the businessman's garden, the loan-shark bent over and picked up two pebbles.

Whilst he was picking them up, the daughter noticed that he'd picked up two black pebbles and placed them both into the bag.

He then asked the daughter to reach into the bag and pick one.

The daughter naturally had only three choices as to what she could have done:

1. *Refuse to pick a pebble from the bag.*
2. *Take both pebbles out of the bag and expose the loan-shark for cheating.*
3. *Pick a pebble from the bag fully well knowing it was black and sacrifice herself for her father's freedom.*

She drew out a pebble from the bag, and before looking at it, she 'accidentally' dropped it into the midst of the other pebbles. She then said to the loan-shark - "Oh, how clumsy of me, but no worries - if you look into the bag for the one that is left, you will be able to tell which pebble I picked."

The pebble left in the bag is obviously black, and seeing as the loan-shark didn't want to be exposed, he had to play along as if the pebble the daughter dropped was white, and clear her father's debt without any marriage.

In this story, we see how the daughter refused the three conventional options at her disposal and thought differently, turning a no-win situation into a huge win. Had she been unable to challenge conventional wisdom and think differently, the businessman would have had a new son-in-law, and the daughter would have lived a miserable life as wife to the loan shark.

We have all heard the phrase, "thinking outside the box." Thinking inside the box is the realm of convention, thinking liking everyone else, lack of imagination and little creativity; thinking outside the box opens up a world of nonconformity, imagination and creativity, defying convention and thinking differently from others. The figurative box is also a barrier – its keeps good ideas in, unable to reach the outside world, while keeping learning out. Ideas are kept in out of fear of being mocked, ridiculed, just being wrong, or having the disappointment of an idea not working. Learning is kept out by a mind not open to the outside, but rather closed off out of fear. By thinking outside of the box… actually, by removing the box from our lives completely, we are opening up the world to our ideas and at the same time opening ourselves to the learning we could never have achieved had we stayed within the box.

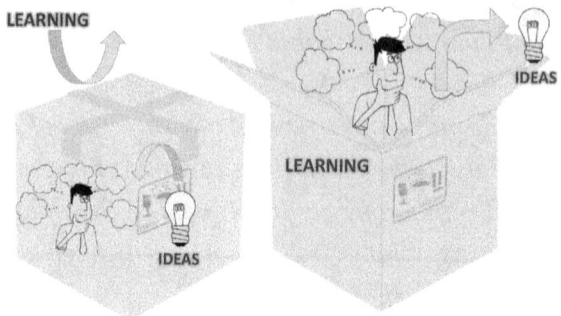

How can we explore, experiment, and experience if we constrain our thinking inside a box?

BREAK THE BOX!

So, let's challenge our ability to think differently, outside the proverbial box, if one still exists in your thinking, by solving this conundrum:

> *You are driving alone in a two-seater car on a deserted road in blizzard conditions, when you see another car which has recently run off the road and into a tree. There are three people in the stranded car, none of whom is injured:*

> - *an old friend, who once saved your life*
> - *your childhood sweetheart & greatest lost love*
> - *an elderly lady*

No-one has a phone. The likelihood of any more passing traffic is effectively zero. The conditions are too dangerous for people to walk anywhere. It is not possible to tow the crashed car. The nearest town is an hour's drive away.

The question is: Given that your car is just a two-seater, in what order should the stranded people be taken to the nearest town?

What's your answer?

Question Everything

Nonconformity is defined as "refusal to conform to an established or conventional creed, rule, or practice" (Merriam-Webster Dictionary). Difference makers call it dissent, conformists call it heresy. The next component in refusing to conform is to question – question traditions, question rules, question strategies, question processes. Questioning is not, as those in power typically claim, subversive or seditious, but rather the ultimate act of loyalty, attempting to improve the current practices of the organization.

Questioning allows us to find flaws, examine weaknesses, and seek improvements in current practices so that we can overcome limitations and exploit opportunities. Elon Musk, the co-founder and CEO of Tesla, Inc., claims the best bit of advice is to ***"constantly think about how you could be doing things better and questioning yourself."*** That goes for your organization, as well. Listen to Einstein and never stop questioning!

"Learn from yesterday, live for today, hope for tomorrow. The important thing is not to stop questioning." _ Albert Einstein

Feed Your Discontent

As Thomas Edison told us, there is no progress without discontent. Satisfaction and complacency give rise to a culture that values the status quo, with a focus on preventing regression rather than pursuing progress. Playing it safe becomes a mantra while change becomes a four-letter word. It is only when there is a feeling of discontent that individuals are motivated to push the envelope, take chances, and drive innovation.

Discontent stimulates creativity and launches an exploration for opportunities, guiding the individual and organization on a journey of discovery. A leader feeds his or her discontent by never settling for where he or she is, constantly questioning why things are the way they are, how they got to be, and how they can be made better - always questioning conventional

A leader feeds his or her discontent by never settling for where he or she is, constantly questioning why things are the way they are, how they got to be, and how they can be made better - always questioning conventional wisdom and challenging the status quo.

wisdom and challenging the status quo. As Edison also said, *"Show me a thoroughly satisfied man and I will show you a failure."*

When we find ourselves content, we begin to think like everyone else and we stop questioning. When we stop questioning, we begin to accept things as they are, settling for what is, rather than 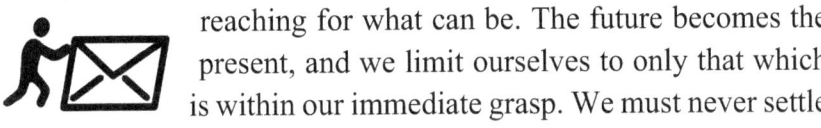 reaching for what can be. The future becomes the present, and we limit ourselves to only that which is within our immediate grasp. We must never settle for what we have already achieved, constantly pushing the envelope forward to progress. Complacency is the death of creativity, innovation, and progress.

"Do we push the envelope on even numbered days and think outside the box on odd or vice versa?"

Thinking differently, questioning, and feeding your discontent are not things you can schedule. You cannot take days off from thinking differently and you cannot turn on a switch and expect that your followers will suddenly challenge the status quo and begin questioning conventional wisdom. It is your responsibility as leader to create an environment in which all members of the organization are comfortable questioning organizational practices, defying logic, and thinking differently. Shouldn't pushing the envelope and thinking outside the box be an everyday expectation?

Think differently, question everything, feed your discontent, and reject conformity, living steadfast in distrust of conventional wisdom and functioning to disrupt the status quo.

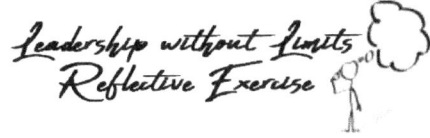

THE NONCONFORMIST IN YOU

Directions: *Choose the statement in column A or B for each item that best describes you. Imagine placing all column A choices you selected on one side of the scale, and all B column choices on the other side of the scale. If A outweighs B, you are more likely to conform. If B outweighs A, then you have the potential to be a nonconformist.*

ITEM	COLUMN A	COLUMN B
1	I prefer to do things the same way they have always been done to maintain satisfactory results.	Even though I have achieved satisfactory results, I like to try new ways of doing things hoping to find better results.
2	I am easily satisfied.	I seem to have trouble finding satisfaction.
3	I don't think of why things are done the way they are in my organization.	I am always questioning why we do the things we do in my organization.
4	I am content to achieve the same results as I have in the past.	I am unhappy if I cannot improve upon past results.
5	I make sure to follow directives without question.	I have a habit of questioning directives to understand why things are done the way they are.

61

Dr. Keith G. Feit

6 Learn to Fail or Fail to Learn

"Every adversity, every failure, every heartache carries with it the seed of an equal or greater benefit."

- Napoleon Hill

Human nature instills in us the desire to always succeed. We see a lack of success as a personal failure, as though we aren't skilled enough or smart enough, to achieve our goal. This mindset leads to a reluctance to tackle challenging tasks, pulling back at the first hint of adversity, and quitting in the face of failure. In short, this mindset leads people down the wrong path, down the path of least resistance and the path of little

> Progress is not possible without the death of the fear of failure and the birth of learning from failure.

accomplishment. Progress is not possible without the death of the fear of failure and the birth of learning from failure. To succeed, we must learn from our failures. Learning from failure allows us to climb the next step toward success; fear of failure prevents us from attempting that step. It's that simple!

"Success is the ability to go from one failure to another with no loss of enthusiasm."
– Winston Churchill

Life is about learning. We learn from everything we do. We learn when we succeed (what works); we learn when we fail (what doesn't work). We learn from every experience, whether good or bad, planned or unplanned, important or unimportant. Famous philosopher and writer, George Santayana, once said, ***"Those who cannot remember the past are condemned to repeat it."*** Not remembering the past is not learning from our mistakes. If we do not learn from our failures, we are ensuring that we will fail again.

> If we do not learn from our failures, we are ensuring that we will fail again.

As failure is critical to our learning of what does not work, providing us a new beginning to find a better way, it is critical for a leader to learn how to fail without giving up. If one does not learn how to fail, and how to learn from such situations, then he or she will always fail to learn. Mistakes are valuable tools if we have the mindset to learn from them. As a leader, you must learn from all experiences, good and bad, and use the new-found wisdom to find a new way to success. Oprah Winfrey put it best, ***"I try to take every***

conflict, every experience, and learn from it. Life is never dull."
This is the attitude of a leader.

 *"Failure is simply the opportunity to begin again, this time more intelligently."* – Henry Ford

When I teach others about the art of leadership, I always try to persuade them that failure is not an end, but a new beginning. As Winston Churchill said, *"Success is not final, failure is not fatal: it is the courage to continue that counts."* Our perception of failure will determine our chances at success… if we view failure as final, in opposition to what Churchill stated, then we are closing the door on success. However, if we see failure as an opportunity to begin again, as Ford pronounced, then we keep that door open waiting for the moment when we can finally walk through to success. Learning from failure is the most powerful learning possible – it lets us know what not to do in order to succeed in the future.

> Failure is not an end, but a new beginning.

"Well, now we know what not to do."

Learning is at the root of personal and organizational growth. If we do not learn, then we do not grow. Without growth, there is no progress. Without progress, there is no positive change. Without positive change, the organization fails, society falters, and we cannot cure the ills of our world. Dramatic? Maybe… but that is how important learning from every experience truly is!

In *Be A Bean*, I proposed that the most important goal of a leader should be to have a positive impact. A leader should make a difference in the lives of others, and he or she plays an important role in making the world a better place, whether for one person, one family, one community, one nation, one race, or the entire world. The only way for a leader to achieve this is to direct the march toward progress, by learning him or herself and fostering an environment where followers learn from their experiences; by growing individually, encouraging the individual growth of others, and promoting organizational growth through learning from failures. Living is learning, and learning is living. We are not experiencing the best of life if we are not learning from our experiences. Learning is what makes life fun and exciting; it makes life worth living. **Leaders must live to learn, and only then do they learn to live.** Once they have mastered the art of living through learning, they can then pass this on to their followers, stimulating the individual and organizational growth required for progress.

> Live to learn and learn to live.

"*Many of life's failures are people who did not realize how close they were to success when they gave up.*"
- Thomas Edison

Churchill is correct that failure is not fatal… unless we allow it to be. Our reaction to failure determines whether or not it is the end or a new beginning. If we bow to the adversity of failing and refuse to fight through to a better ending, than we are choosing not to grow. By choosing to ignore the lessons of failure, we are failing to learn, and this lack of growth resulting from the fear of accepting our inadequacies leads to a dead end in which success is but a distant dream. History is littered with great men and women who endured failure to ultimately find success. The world would be a much different place if these individuals did not learn from their failures and persist in their endeavors. What do I mean?

"I have not failed. I have just found 10,000 ways that won't work." Those are the words of Thomas Edison, inventor of the light bulb. It might be over the top to say the world would have remained in darkness if not for Edison, but the progress that brought civilization light from electricity came from his attitude that he had never failed. He simply learned from each iteration that did not work until he finally found one that did!

"If you're going through hell, keep going." Winston Churchill said this in the 1940s, when he led the British against Hitler's Nazi war machine, and Britain was all that stood between freedom and a world of Nazi "perverted science." Churchill learned from his previous failures that earned him a reputation as an eccentric drunk who was a failure in politics and a warmonger, and he persisted through some of the most significant military failures in world history, to rally the British people to a seemingly impossible resistance of Nazi Germany. If not for Churchill being named prime minister of Great

Britain, and successfully learning from failure, the world could have had a much more Nazi tilt.

"We should not look back unless it is to derive useful lessons from past errors, and for the purpose of profiting by dearly bought experience." An eloquent statement from an eloquent  leader, George Washington led the United States of America to independence on a solid foundation of failure. He famously lost more battles than he won, but he was a man who learned through failure and persistently found ways to alter the battlefield in response to previous mistakes, gaining advantage and ultimately winning the war.

"Success is a lousy teacher. It seduces smart people into thinking they can't lose."
- Bill Gates

Tying learning how to fail with learning from failure requires that a person learn how to reflect. Reflection involves a deep, introspective look within – Who you are, why you did what you did, what was effective, what was ineffective, other possible ways to approach the situation in the future, things you need to change… just to begin. The most important thing to remember is that failure is life's great teacher… it's ok to fail into success!

Live to learn and learn to live by conquering the fear of failure and utilizing failure as a learning opportunity.

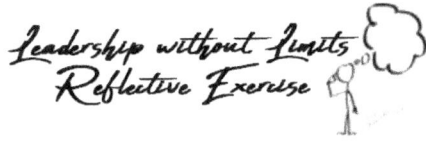

DO YOU LIVE TO LEARN?

1. What is the first thing you think about when you make a mistake or your effort fails?

2. How often do you reflect on your successes and failures?

3. Outline your reflection practice (Explain how you reflect).

4. What questions do you ask yourself when you reflect? How honest are you in answering those questions?

"IT'S IMPOSSIBLE TO LIVE WITHOUT FAILING AT SOMETHING UNLESS YOU LIVE SO CAUTIOUSLY THAT YOU MIGHT AS WELL NOT HAVE LIVED AT ALL, IN WHICH CASE YOU HAVE FAILED BY DEFAULT."

- J. K. Rowling

7 Empower Your Superheroes

"Leaders become great, not because of their power, but because of their ability to empower others."

— John Maxwell

Leaders have power over others, whether formal power of their position within an organization, informal power of their personal influence and interpersonal relationships, or expert power due to their knowledge and skill. Power is a mighty instrument of accomplishment. It can be used for good, but more often has been used for bad. Those leaders who lead to promote their own self-interests, those we call self-servant leaders, are puppet masters, pulling the strings of their followers to ensure the leader's personal priorities are addressed. There is little, if any, freedom offered to subordinates and

> Self-servant leaders covet power for their own enrichment; servant leaders seek power to empower others.

empowerment is non-existent. On the other end of the spectrum, with those leaders who promote the interests of the organization over their own personal interests, there is regular empowerment of organizational members with individuals freed to take initiative and pursue opportunities without the direction of a superior. Self-servant leaders covet power for their own enrichment; servant leaders seek power to empower

> The star of a self-servant leader burns very bright, but also burns out very quickly. The empowerment that occurs under the administrate of a servant leader allows the star of that leader to sustain its sparkle long after his or her reign has passed.

others. For this reason, the star of a self-servant leader burns very bright, but also burns out very quickly. The empowerment that occurs under the administrate of a servant leader allows the star of that leader to sustain its sparkle long after his or her reign has passed.

 VS.

Self-servant Leader

- Organizational goals promote leader's interests
- Employees lack freedom
- Empowerment is artificial
- Employees serve interests of leader

Servant Leader

- Leader's goals promote organization's interests
- Employees granted autonomy
- True empowerment
- Leader serves interests of employees

Bill Gates, founder and CEO of Microsoft, claims that, *"As we look ahead to the next century, leaders will be those who empower others."* It is through empowerment that individual commitment is gained, progress is made, and organizations move forward.

> *"If your actions inspire others to dream more, learn more, do more, and become more, you are a leader."* – John Quincy Adams

As a leader, you are tasked with finding ways to motivate your followers to commit to the cause, to encourage them to take initiative, and to inspire them to achieve more than they thought possible. Empowerment occurs not only by the extension of an opportunity to followers to make decisions and take actions, but also by fostering a culture and climate where they are comfortable taking such chances. It is important to remember that empowerment only occurs when opportunity meets desire. If individuals do not have the desire or motivation to make decisions and take actions, then empowering them to do so is not only a wasted effort, but can actually have negative consequences.

> It is important to remember that empowerment only occurs when opportunity meets desire.

In the world of fantasy and science fiction that so many of us enjoy reading and watching, civilization often survives thanks to the supernatural powers of one or more superheroes – Superman, Wonder Woman, The Avengers, etc. These superheroes face down the evil, seemingly unstoppable power of the villains, ultimately defeating their foes and saving humanity from subservience or extinction. How does this relate to real life?

Leaders have superheroes at their fingertips every single day. External menaces threaten the organization on a near daily basis. Internal threats lurk around every corner. A leader alone, regardless of how smart or skilled, cannot keep the enemies of success at bay. The future of the organization is in the hands of your employees. These are your superheroes, and it is only through the empowerment granted from you, the leader, that they have the power to defeat the threats, promote progress, and ensure the survival and success of the organization into the future.

"If I have seen further than others it is by standing on the shoulders of giants."
- Sir Isaac Newton

It is critical to remember that no one achieves anything in isolation and of only their own abilities. Success requires the combined efforts of many, especially when we are talking about the success of an organization. We all stand on shoulders at some point in our lives, we all need others' support, and we all need to supplement our talents with the talents of others. A leader who suppresses his followers' creativity and proactive innovativeness, and gains compliance through fear, is disempowering his employees to the point of organizational fragility. This fragility stems from the lack of commitment from followers and a workforce that has not been empowered to tackle problems and exploit opportunities. The organization then becomes reactive, only acting at the directive of the leadership. Temporary success is thus fragile, capable of morphing into organizational dysfunction and failure at the slightest hint of adversity. A leader who empowers his followers, fostering a culture that encourages and promotes creativity and innovation, is creating a sustainable structure for organizational growth and success. In such an environment, employees are free to take the initiative to head off potential complications before they become problematic, and to proactively seek out and exploit opportunities without the shackles of asking for permission. Thus, these organizations are strong, stable, and agile, built not only for success in the present environment, but adaptable and flexible enough to continue winning in the future.

> A leader who empowers his followers, fostering a culture that encourages and promotes creativity and innovation, is creating a sustainable structure for organizational growth and success.

> "It is not the strongest of the species that survives, nor the most intelligent that survives. It is the one that is most adaptable to change." – Charles Darwin

As I was taught by my mentor, Dr. John Pisapia, agility, for both individual leaders and organizations, is incredibly important in the constantly changing, chaotic, and ambiguous environments of the postmodern condition. Flexibility and adaptability are critical if one is to successfully navigate the minefields of the highly competitive globally interconnected markets of the 21st Century. These components of successful leadership and organizational triumph sprout when individuals' comfort zones expand and they feel more freedom to take chances and change on the fly.

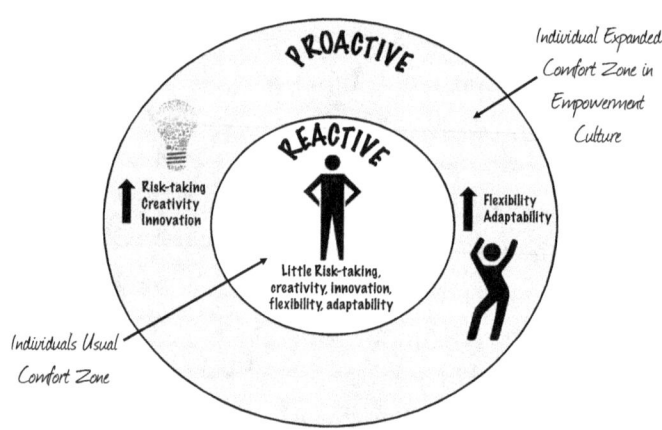

How Can I Empower My Followers?

Empowerment grows first from a culture and climate that invites individuals to engage in risk-taking while taking the initiative to solve problems and exploit opportunities, all of their own volition. Such a culture is one that values creativity and innovation, promotes and encourages proactive behavior, and celebrates failures as learning opportunities. In such a culture, setbacks are not frowned upon, and successes, while celebrated, are not dwelled upon. These cultures, by the power of their forgiving and supportive natures, actually expand the comfort zones of individual members of the organization. I call organizations that have such cultures **empowerment zones**.

The establishment of an empowerment zone and the culture we just discussed cannot come to fruition without the development of strong interpersonal relationships. Stronger relationships mean more trust, greater levels of respect, and increased personal loyalties between members of the organization and the leadership. It is the leader's job to build these relationships by supporting rather than undermining, helping instead of abandoning, and praising in place of berating. Too many leaders undermine their followers by passing blame, even more turn their backs on those who are struggling, and with even more we often hear criticism over compliments. Leaders build strong relationships, fostering trust and promoting mutual respect, by allowing followers the freedom to fail, by providing assistance to followers who struggle rather than turning their back and terminating employment, by owning mistakes and protecting

> Followers need to believe in their hearts that they have a leader who has their back, who they feel is always in their corner, and one that they can always count on – one who is authentic, transparent, and a person of unquestioned integrity.

followers from internal and external pressures, and by rebuking in private and praising in public. Followers need to believe in their hearts that they have a leader who has their back, who they feel is always in their corner, and one that they can always count on – one who is authentic, transparent, and a person of unquestioned integrity.

As the culture and relationships are continuously being developed, it becomes necessary to evaluate the workforce to determine who has particular skills, attributes, and expertise to help the leadership move the organization forward. To successfully empower others, a leader must know his or her people, being sure to put each individual in a position to succeed. By taking the time to learn about his or her followers, a leader can most effectively determine to whom certain tasks should be delegated. Delegating a task that does not fit an individual's strengths sets that person up for failure and squashes his or her motivation to accept empowerment. The leader risks alienating that individual, destroying any trust that had developed and lessening respect for the leader. The more this happens, the more people will talk, and the greater the probability of the development of a toxic climate.

> Delegating a task that does not fit an individual's strengths sets that person up for failure and squashes his or her motivation to accept empowerment.

Delegation can occur after proper evaluation of personnel. As a leader relinquishes control of important aspects of an organization, he or she empowers those who have been tasked with those essential decisions and tasks. The most effective leaders are those who are confident enough in their own abilities and sure enough in their standing to let go of the reins, to offer more freedom, and to relinquish power to those within the organization. The more power is distributed throughout the organization, rather than consolidated in a single leader, the more agile an organization will be, better structured to adapt to changes in the external environment and flexible enough to maneuver past internal problems.

> "The really expert riders of horses let the horse know immediately who is in control, but then guide the horse with loose reins and seldom use the spurs." – Sandra Day O'Connor

When tasks are delegated, it is necessary to ensure those newly empowered individuals are supported in every way. This support could be in the form of material resources, additional personnel, or advice, among others. Empowerment does not mean abdication of leadership. The leader must remain actively involved in delegation by constantly monitoring the situation without micromanaging. **The key is to balance the assistance offered between the assistance requested, which will be considered support, and the assistance you desire, which could be considered micromanaging.**

> Empowerment does not mean abdication of leadership.

It is a delicate balance between true empowerment with support and delegation with micromanagement. As with everything a leader does, empowerment must be authentic, support must be real, and trust must remain unfettered. There is no room in leadership for masks and disguises; followers need to know who it is that they are following – they can't be expected to trust a stranger or respect someone who tries to be someone he or she isn't.

When we talk about micromanagement and abdication of leadership, neither one is worse than the other. Each leads to a corrosion of confidence in leadership and a toxic climate permeating the organization. Micromanaging reduces trust, as leaders are clearly demonstrating their perceived need to control the actions of their subordinates, unwilling or unable to let go of the reins. If an individual feels as

> It is a delicate balance between true empowerment with support and delegation with micromanagement.

though he or she is simply serving as a vessel of the leader, without the ability to act freely, the result will be compliance, weak in its effect, rather than the powerful act of commitment. Alas, nothing brews bad blood between leader and follower quicker than delegating a task followed by the leader assuming control via the back door of micromanagement – it is a strategy that puts the leader in position to assume credit for a success while deflecting blame for a failure, and everyone knows it… This is the classic case of throwing a follower under the bus!

The other end of the spectrum is no better. Abdicating your role as leader causes just as much damage as being too involved. How can your people believe in you if you are afraid to make decisions and take action? Again, this lessens trust and absolutely destroys the level of respect for the leader. As much as they sometimes might not want to admit it, followers need a leader to take control, to assure them in difficult times, and to calmly navigate the organization through crisis situations. I have worked for a leader who actually manages to micromanage while abdicating leadership – I don't know how, but I have seen that it actually happens – and trust me, the culture and climate under such leadership could not be any more toxic… no trust, no respect, no loyalty, no happiness!

Former West Virginia governor and current U.S. Senator Joe Manchin declared, **"I would never abdicate, nor would I expect any other governor to abdicate, the responsibility to protect the people of my state."** This should be a leader's creed – he or she should never abdicate the responsibility of protecting his or her people and the organization they have been entrusted to guide. A large part of this responsibility is to make the tough decisions that may not be popular and to take actions that may seem unconventional.

As with everything a leader does, empowerment must be authentic, support must be real, and trust must remain unfettered.

Obviously, not all tasks delegated will go exactly as planned or turn out positively, even without micromanagement or abdication. In those situations, in which there is success, those successes should be celebrated and those responsible should be praised. In those situations, where the results are less than satisfactory, those disappointing results must be acknowledged, and an immediate collaborative effort should be implemented to improve the outcomes.

When there is failure, it is critical to keep the empowered individual involved in the corrective action, and to follow the better results with praise. Unfortunately, poor outcomes can't always be rectified, and in such a situation a leader can't be all sunshine and rainbows. Sometimes it becomes necessary to lay down the hammer – reprimand, penance, and if need be, termination.

True empowerment comes with the distribution of credit. Nothing does more damage more quickly than a leader who takes credit from his or her followers. It might not seem fair, but a leader must freely give away credit for successes and loyally assume blame for failures (to an extent!). You want to provide as much cover as possible for good employees, even if you need to take a hit. In the end, standing up for followers will earn you greater trust and respect, and foster a culture in which they feel more empowered to try new things and take chances. This does not mean covering for incompetence, or brushing aside actions that require attention, but providing cover and support for temporary lapses or mistakes. A leader cannot do it alone and should never act as though he or she can. He or she needs an empowered workforce to realize the vision of the organization. **Share the wealth of recognition; share the praise for a job well done; share the future of your organization with all members.**

"No man will make a great leader who wants to do it all himself or get all the credit for doing it.
- Andrew Carnegie

> Empowerment generates flexibility and adaptability that allow an organization to effectively navigate change.

Leaders empower others because an empowered membership is the best strategy for organizational success and the best protection against institutional failure. Empowerment generates the flexibility and adaptability that allow an organization to effectively navigate change. Greater empowerment also reduces weaknesses within the organization by providing effective leadership at all levels and in all departments.

Remember, it doesn't matter who fails, or where that failure occurs within the organization... we sink or swim together!

Relinquish power and empower others by building strong interpersonal relationships formed in the spirit of trust and mutual respect.

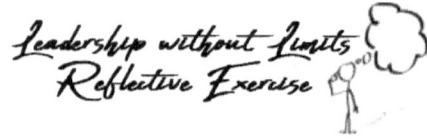

Leadership without Limits
Reflective Exercise

DO WE HAVE AN EMPOWERMENT ZONE?

Directions: *Describe the main characteristics of your culture in the blank diagram below.*

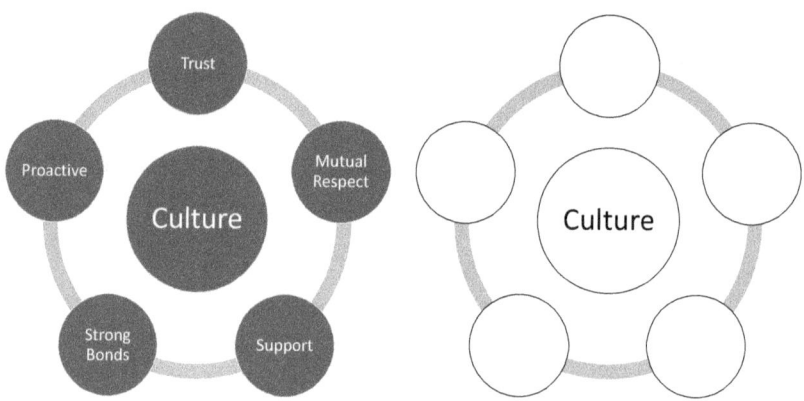

1. Does your organizational culture support empowerment? Why or why not? If not, what can you do to create an empowerment zone?

2. Reflect back on times when you delegated tasks to subordinates. Did you support or micromanage? How do you know the difference?

"A leader is best when people barely know he exists, when his work is done, his aim fulfilled, they will say: We did it ourselves."

- Lao Tzu

8 Establish Your Dream Team

"The strength of the team is each individual member. The strength of
each member is the team."

– Phil Jackson

We have already read about the importance of a leader
realizing and understanding that he or she cannot succeed alone. An
effective leader is one who builds an effective team. The hiring of
personnel that fits the organizational culture and is willing to
sacrifice for the attainment of organizational goals, while having the
necessary talents and abilities, is of paramount importance.
Although leaders typically keep their eyes on the best and brightest,
it is often necessary to look deeper for those individual who have
specific talents, skills, or attributes that the organization lacks. There
are different thoughts regarding the building of the organization's

"roster." Some look for individuals with specific abilities to work in select departments while others simply look for the best candidates, worrying about finding a position to fit their abilities later. How you put your team together depends on what is important to you, the purpose of your organization, the type of employees you are looking for, and the role you envision for your new hires. If you have a specific system where certain skills are required in different departments, then you would likely look for individuals who possess that required skill set. If, however, yours is a more general structure that does not require specific skills for individual departments, then you might take a best and brightest approach, assigning roles and responsibilities after hiring.

"The first method for estimating the intelligence of a ruler is to look at the men he has around him."
- Niccolo Machiavelli

Regardless of how the rank and file of an organization are hired and positioned, a leader must find his or her way to a dynamic leadership team. A good leadership rule of thumb is to heed the words of Steve Jobs, *"Great things in business are never done by one person. They're done by a team of people."* These are wise words not only in the business world, but in any profession. Never try to do it all yourself, never chase glory, never cast blame, and never forget why you put the team together in the first place – it's about what's best for the organization.

In building a team, the leader shares the burdens of leadership, which are far too great for any one individual, and offers credit and praise for triumphs while securing a support structure for challenging times, and a safety net for failures. The more a team operates as one, the more they will come to believe that they are all parts of a greater "one," and blame and negativity will be overpowered by trust and support.

"It is amazing what you can achieve if you do not mind who gets the credit." – Harry Truman

What Makes An Effective Team?

There are certain aspects of a team that determine its capacity for effectiveness. A homogenous leadership team is not desirable in the least, as similar experiences, perspectives, and talents will lead to the quickest decisions and consensus-based solutions, but these will not be the wisest decisions and best solutions. In any endeavor, it makes sense that you would want to surround yourself with others who have ideas and opinions different than your own, and unique talents that can offset any of your weaknesses. In short, you want the best and brightest, even if… no, especially, if they do not always agree with you.

The best example of this is Abraham Lincoln's team of rivals, his presidential cabinet constructed in 1860. Lincoln took William Seward as his secretary of state, Salmon Chase as his secretary of the treasury, Edward Bates as his attorney general, and eventually Edwin Stanton as his secretary of war, during the American Civil War. This was extraordinary in that Lincoln did not have any personal or professional connection to any of them, and none had any loyalty to Lincoln or commitment to his agenda. In fact, each of these individuals, with the exception of Stanton, was his rival for the Republican presidential nomination that year. Lincoln's goals, however, were to keep the party together and construct the best team for the country. His reasoning in his own words, ***"We need the strongest men of the party in the Cabinet. We needed to hold our own people together. I had looked the party over and concluded that these were the very strongest men. Then I had no right to deprive the country of their services."*** Just as Lincoln had no right to deprive the country of the most capable leaders of the day due to ideological or personal differences, so too do you not have the right to deprive your organization of the best men and women to guide it due to personal differences or varying opinions.

An effective team requires its members to have:

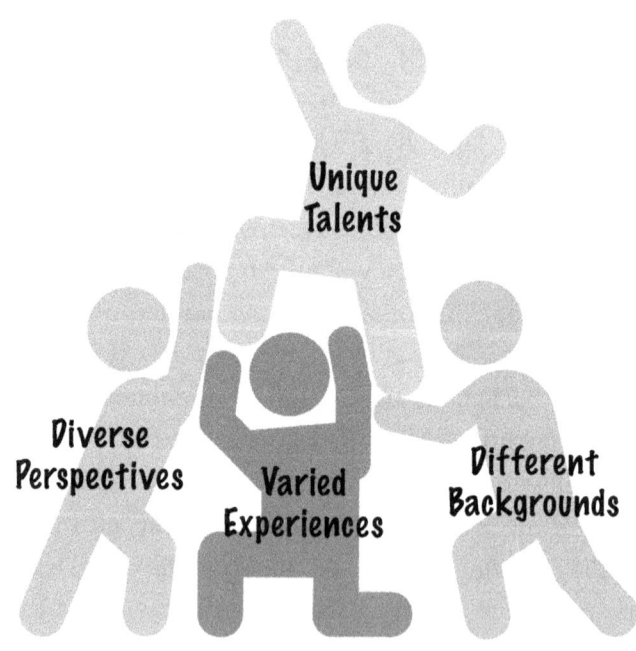

It is important for teams to consist of diverse individuals with differing backgrounds, experiences, perspectives, personalities, and talents. Diversity is not just about race, ethnicity, and gender, although these are important components. The more diverse the team, the greater the spectrum of opinions and ideas will be available. It makes sense that individuals from different cultures, who grew up in different regions or neighborhoods, and have taken different paths to where they currently find themselves, would have a broad range of perspectives on most issues. This range affords the team a wide variety of options as they seek to come to the best decision or most effective solution.

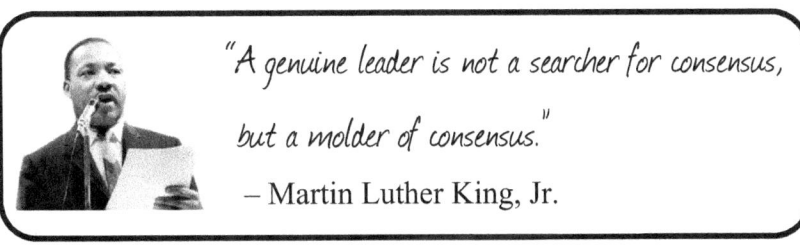

"A genuine leader is not a searcher for consensus, but a molder of consensus."

– Martin Luther King, Jr.

How Does An Effective Team Work?

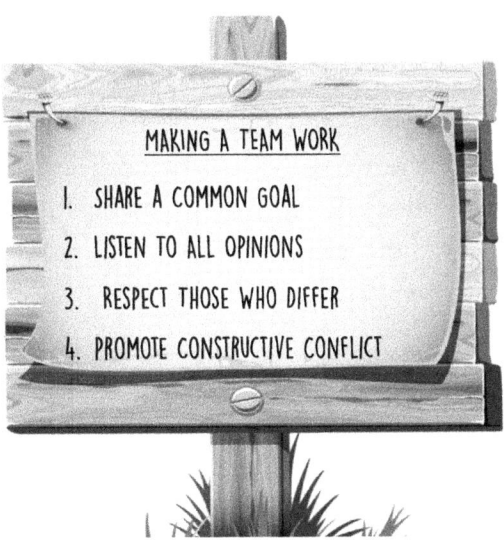

MAKING A TEAM WORK

1. SHARE A COMMON GOAL
2. LISTEN TO ALL OPINIONS
3. RESPECT THOSE WHO DIFFER
4. PROMOTE CONSTRUCTIVE CONFLICT

Share A Common Goal

An effective team needs something that binds them together in both thought and action. Why should people with different opinions and ideas negotiate, compromise, and sometimes bend to the will of others? There is no reason unless there is a common goal that informs the decision-making process, a goal so important to all members that pride does not overpower the desire for an effective outcome. When all minds are aligned in pursuit of the common goal, individuals are willing to let go of some control, and compromise, with the assumption that compromise will lead to a more desired result and better outcomes for the organization.

Listen to All Opinions

When all members of a team are aligned in their desire to achieve a common goal, the rest comes easier. Now, it doesn't make any sense to have varying experiences, diverse perspectives, and unique talents among the team members if they are not going to be utilized. Thus, it is imperative that ALL opinions are not only heard, but listened to. There are no instances in which any team member should have their input ignored, and every word spoken amongst team members must be heard and considered. The best decisions and most effective solutions are usually a combination of ideas from multiple members of the team, so a leader ignores the input of team members at his or her own peril.

Respect Those Who Differ

Part of listening to all opinions is maintaining respect for those opinions or ideas that differ from yours. These differences are what makes a team strong. These differences are the critical component of arriving at the best outcome. A leader who does not respect the suggestions of all members and ensure that all members are respecting each other's opinions and ideas, is a leader who will soon find that he or she has lost the team. This is ineffective leadership that can cause the development of a toxic culture and allows negativity and doubt to pervade the organization. It is critical to always remember that respect, much as trust, is a two-way street. A leader cannot earn the respect of followers if he or she does not demonstrate an equal level of respect for the followers. Any lack of trust or respect is a crack in the armor of an organization, and this crack grows with each negative message that is passed from one member to another. It's a heck of a lot easier to lose trust then it is to earn it, and once it is lost it is extremely difficult to regain. So don't do anything to lose it! Always respect all!

Promote Constructive Conflict

Finally, the best outcome is one that consists of a conglomeration of the ideas and opinions shared between team members. As Martin Luther King, Jr. said, a leader should not look for consensus, but build consensus. The leader needs to ignite constructive conflict amongst team members. Unlike destructive conflict, which fosters ill will and the development of a toxic culture, constructive conflict involves members offering differing ideas and opinions, respecting the input of others, and evaluating and debating ideas according to their potential to help the team achieve its common goal. When individuals can offer

> When individuals can offer contrasting and sometimes competing ideas in a calm, respectful dialogue, the team can increase productivity and advance the organization toward reaching its goals.

contrasting and sometimes competing ideas in a calm, respectful dialogue, the team can increase productivity and advance the organization toward reaching its goals.

Destructive Conflict   Constructive Conflict

- Individuals look for personal gain
- Conversations become personal
- Ideas shared to convince others
- Positive gains not realized
- Members block each other from progress
- Fosters negative climate and toxic culture

- Individuals work for mutual gain
- Conversations remain professional
- Ideas shared to find best solution
- Positive gains realized and celebrated
- Members aid each other's progress
- Forster positive climate and supportive culture

In an interview, Steve Jobs shared a metaphor for the importance of constructive conflict,

> "...what I've always felt that a team of people doing something they really believe in is like when I was a young kid and there was a widowed man that lived up the street. He was in his eighties. He was a little scary looking. And I got to know him a little bit. I think he may have paid me to mow his lawn or something.

> "One day he said to me, 'Come in into my garage, I want to show you something.' And he pulled out this dusty old rock tumbler. It was a motor and a coffee can and a little band between them. And he said,

'come with me.' We went out into the back and we got just some rocks... some regular old ugly rocks. And we put them in the can with a little bit of liquid and little bit of grit powder, and we closed the can up and he turned this motor on and he said, 'come back tomorrow,,.' *and this can was making a racket as the stones went around.*

And I came back the next day, and we opened the can. And we took out these amazingly beautiful polished rocks. The same common stones that had gone in, through rubbing against each other like this (Jobs clapped his hands), creating a little bit of friction, creating a little bit of noise, had come out these beautiful polished rocks.

That's always been in my mind my metaphor for a team working really hard on something they're passionate about.

It's that through the team, through that group of incredibly talented people bumping up against each other, having arguments, having fights sometimes, making some noise, and working together they polish each other and they polish the ideas, and what comes out are these really beautiful stones."

The importance of the noise, disagreement and friction that come from constructive conflict seems to be clear, but the question a leader faces is, how do we promote constructive conflict without also giving rise to destructive conflict?

How Can We Promote Constructive Conflict?

In order to engage in constructive conflict, individuals need to learn about their colleagues, learn to communicate positively, and understand differences. The more your team understands the differences that exist, and the more they know about each other, the greater the environment exists for the development of strong interpersonal relationships. We can learn about and from each other, developing trust and respect along the way, through team-building exercises. These can occur at annual or semi-annual retreats, or simply through weekly or monthly meetings, but it is important to engage your team in as many opportunities to build a reliance on each other as possible. Through these activities, members learn about each other's strengths, gain respect for their peers, and build levels of trust that will be necessary for organizational growth and success.

Another key to building an effective team is effectual communication. Communication is critical in all aspects of life, but especially in the promotion of constructive conflict. Individuals must learn how to speak in a manner that is inclusive and not exclusive, as well as informative rather than directive. Sharing ideas and opinions for the good of the organization is optimal, but if other members feel as though they are being told what to do or talked down to, the desired effect will be lost in translation.

> Individuals must learn how to speak in a manner that is inclusive and not exclusive, as well as informative rather than directive.

> It is critical that all members learn how to be active listeners, truly hearing what is being said when others speak, engaged in the conversation when they are not speaking, and showing respect for each individual as it becomes his or her turn to share.

Along with learning how to speak, it is critical that all members learn how to be active listeners, truly hearing what is being said when others speak, engaged in the conversation when they are not speaking, and showing respect for each individual as it becomes his or her turn to share. Active listening means actually listening to and hearing what the individual is saying, not preparing a rebuttal in your head as he or she is speaking.

Differing from destructive conflict, where communication is designed to persuade others to side with an individual's personal agenda, communication in constructive conflict is meant to present different perspectives, opinions, and ideas, offering these as possible options in creating the best outcome. Propositions must be communicated in a positive manner, not as a win-lose proposition for the individual, and communication must never be aimed at the personal expense of any colleague.

How about meetings?

Meetings are a tool of effective leadership if, and only if, they are conducted as needed, conducted efficiently, and conducted with a purpose. First, meetings should only be held when important decisions require direct input and debate, and information cannot be disseminated by other means. Too many meetings, as well as what are perceived as needless meetings, are a recipe for a disgruntled membership at best, and a full blown mutiny at worst. Patrick

Lencioni wrote a book entitled, *Death By Meeting*, which is an accurate way to describe the agony members of an organization feel when they have to sit through monotonous meetings that seem to have no reason, no order, and no end. I came by a quote with an unknown author one day, and it pops to the forefront of my mind every time I sit in a meeting – "A meeting is an event at which the minutes are kept and the hours are lost." Just think about the hours that are lost, in some cases, each and every day!

> A meeting is an event at which the minutes are kept and the hours are lost.

Management expert Peter Drucker doesn't sound like a strong supporter of meetings, saying, ***"Meetings are by definition a concession to deficient organizations. For one either meets or works."*** Unfortunately, too many times we take people away from important work to waste their time in meetings. Again, meetings can be an important aspect of successful leadership, but only when limited, necessary, and productive.

"I know we didn't get anything accomplished,
but that's what meetings are for."

Meetings must be organized with discipline maintained in order to be productive. This requires the introduction of norms for every meeting. These norms should be discussed with the members and decided on collaboratively so that everyone has buy-in. The established norms should guide every meeting, no matter duration, purpose, or attendees. Norms can include how members will participate, what is expected of an individual's participation, time restrictions, or other aspects as determined important by the team. An example of meeting norms is below:

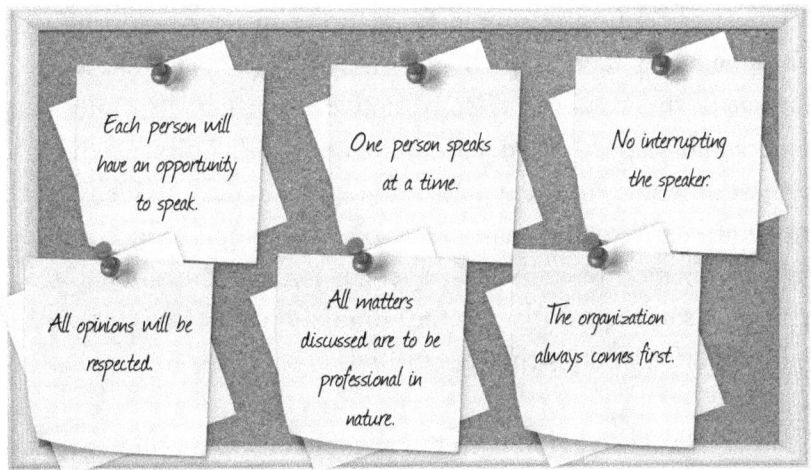

There are no right and wrong norms. They are for you and your team to decide. Just make sure that the norms of meetings align with the shared values and beliefs of the organization, that they are determined collaboratively, and that they guide each and every meeting once they are adopted. If norms are not implemented regularly and without fail, then they simply become irrelevant, lacking the authority to maintain order in meetings. It is also very important that the team determines the norms. As with everything, the best way to gain buy-in is for everyone involved to have ownership.

"Peace is not absence of conflict, it is the ability to handle conflict by peaceful means.
- Ronald Reagan

It is important for a leader to remember that conflict will always exist, both within the organization and beyond its outermost walls. There will, and should be, conflict in every meeting, with every decision, and with every strategy. The substance of the conflict is the key – is it constructive, focusing on professional matters and respectfully debating the opinions of all, searching for the best outcome for the organization? Or is it destructive, with the intrusion of personal attacks, disrespecting of opposing views, and the prioritization of individual agendas over organizational goals? What needs to be prioritized is the elimination of destructive conflict and promotion of constructive conflict.

Let me leave you with this parable of the six blind men and the elephant:

> *Six blind men were discussing exactly what they believed an elephant to be, since each had heard how strange the creature was, yet none had ever seen one before. So the blind men agreed to find an elephant and discover what the animal was really like. It didn't take the blind men long to find an elephant at a nearby market.*

The first blind man approached the beast and felt the animal's firm flat side. "It seems to me that the elephant is just like a wall," he said to his friends.

The second blind man reached out and touched one of the elephant's tusks. "No, this is round and smooth and sharp - the elephant is like a spear."

Intrigued, the third blind man stepped up to the elephant and touched its trunk. "Well, I can't agree with either of you; I feel a squirming writhing thing - surely the elephant is just like a snake."

The fourth blind man was of course by now quite puzzled. So he reached out, and felt the elephant's leg. "You are all talking complete nonsense," he said, "because clearly the elephant is just like a tree."

Utterly confused, the fifth blind man stepped forward and grabbed one of the elephant's ears. "You must all be mad - an elephant is exactly like a fan."

Duly, the sixth man approached, and, holding the beast's tail, disagreed again. "It's nothing like any of your descriptions - the elephant is just like a rope."

And all six blind men continued to argue, based on their own particular experiences, as to what they thought an elephant was like. It was an argument that they were never able to resolve. Each of them was concerned only with their own idea. None of them had the full picture, and none could see any of the other's point of view. Each man saw the elephant as something quite different, and while in part each blind man was right, none was wholly correct.

If members of the team are not listening to each other and respecting what each has to say, but rather each is anchored in their own thoughts, opinions, and ideas, then the team will never come to the right conclusion about what an elephant is (best decision, most effective solution, or most promising idea).

Develop a dynamic team within a culture that values diverse perspectives, respects opposing views, and promotes constructive conflict.

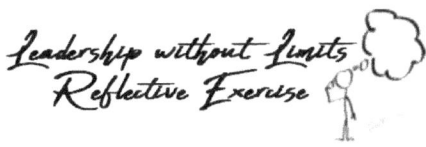

Leadership without limits
Reflective Exercise

IS MY TEAM DYNAMIC?

1. Who do you consider a part of your leadership team? Why are each of these individuals on your team? What makes each of them a valued member?

2. Of the conflict occurring within your organization, what percentage is constructive and what percentage is destructive?

3. Reflect back on your meetings... Are all members invited to share ideas? Are all opinions heard and respected? How are competing ideas debated? Do members attempt to persuade or contribute?

4. Think about how you can improve your leadership team. Are there specific perspectives missing? Does anyone have particular expertise that can help the team? Can you implement norms to ensure constructive conflict?

9 Get to Know Who's in the Mirror

"He who conquers others is strong; He who conquers himself is mighty."

- Lao Tzu

To lead others, one must first find the path to leading oneself. A leader first must accept who he or she is before promoting his or her leadership to others. This seems to be a relatively simple task, but to truly know and understand yourself, and to accept who you are, blemishes and all, is very difficult. There are many reasons that people refuse to acknowledge their true self, sometimes intentionally from conscious decisions, and sometimes unintentionally from the

> Without overcoming the fear of facing who you are, you can never become who you are destined to be.

subconscious. The truth is, without overcoming the fear of facing who you are, you can never become who you are destined to be.

Why are some individuals so afraid of letting the world see the real them?

Whatever the reasons for putting on the mask of a stranger, every bit of your true self that you hide from others, and from yourself, the weaker you are as a leader. Authenticity is critical to leader and follower coming together – it is the foundation of the trust, respect, and loyalty that builds the strong interpersonal relationships on which a successful organization thrives. In an earlier chapter we discussed the need to remove all disguises. Once again, all masks must be removed, any facades need to be replaced with the true self, and you need to reconcile those less desirable fragments of who

> Authenticity is critical to leader and follower coming together – it is the foundation of the trust, respect, and loyalty that builds the strong interpersonal relationships on which a successful organization thrives.

you are with the characteristics of the person you need, or want, to become.

The truth is, there is often a battle between different versions of oneself. There can many times be a struggle between the self you want to be and the self you have shown to the world, or between the self you need to be and the self you have so far been. How do you ensure the self you need and want wins the battle and is your true self? Take a look at the parable, *The Two Wolves*:

An old Cherokee chief was teaching his grandson about life...

"A fight is going on inside me," he said to the boy. "It is a terrible fight and it is between two wolves.

"One is evil - he is anger, envy, sorrow, regret, greed, arrogance, self-pity, guilt, resentment, inferiority, lies, false pride, superiority, self-doubt, and ego.

The other is good - he is joy, peace, love, hope, serenity, humility, kindness, benevolence, empathy, generosity, truth, compassion, and faith.

This same fight is going on inside you - and inside every other person, too."

The grandson thought about it for a minute and then asked his grandfather, "Which wolf will win?"

The old chief simply replied, "The one you feed."

As the old chief says, you determine who you are and who you show yourself to be to the world. The one you feed, meaning the one owning the values you demonstrate will be the one the world sees. Whether that is the good wolf or the bad wolf, that is something you must decide; you are the only one who has the power to determine which wolf wins.

Below is a copy of a slide I use in my leadership workshop, when I ask each participant to define themselves by looking into the mirror and answering these questions honestly. This definition of who you are is critical if you are to present an authentic leader to your organization… without authenticity,

> Every bit of your true self that you hide from others, and from yourself, the weaker you are as a leader.

followers will find it difficult to respect and support your leadership.

 **PREPARE** **Before you can realize your potential as a leader, you first must define who you are…**

What is important to me?

Why do you do what you do? What drives you? What are your expectations, standards, goals? What motivates you?

What do I stand for?

What is important to you? For what are you willing to sacrifice? What are you willing to sacrifice?

Who do I serve?

Do you serve others? If so, who? Or do you serve your own interests? Greater good or self promotion?

What can I do?

Can you change who you are? Can you learn more? Can you improve your skills? Can you get better?

Who controls my outcomes?

Do you control the outcomes of your decisions and actions or are those outcomes out of your control?

The members of your organization and any external agent important to the functioning of your organization in the marketplace, must understand the following about you:

1. What drives you?
2. What do you stand for?

3. Who do you serve?
4. What are you capable of?
5. Are you in control?

What drives you?

The first step in understanding who you are as a leader is to recognize what it is that drives you. Why is it that you do what you do? If you do not know why you do the things you do, then you will have little motivation to persist when things get tough. If you do not have a true understanding of what it is that's important to you, then what is it you are trying to achieve? Internal motivation is driven by what is important to you, what you desire to achieve; if there is no end in sight, then where

> Internal motivation is driven by what is important to you, what you desire to achieve.

are you going? Before  embarking on your journey, you must determine the finish line… in other words, why are you doing what you are doing and where do you want to go?

What do you stand for?

Speaking of what is important to you, what do you stand for? Are you a cold-hearted businessman whose only concern is the bottom line, where company revenue and market share are more important than employees' lives? Are you a humanitarian leader who worries about the well-being of each individual member of the organization at the expense of outcomes?

To find out what you stand for, you first have to figure out what is important to you. Once you have determined that, think about what you would be willing to sacrifice for. As a principal, would you be willing to sacrifice short-term test scores to support a teacher implementing an innovative strategy that holds the promise of future increases in student achievement? As a CEO of a company, would you be willing to sacrifice your job to do what was morally right? Would you be willing to bear the brunt of ridicule or your own good fortune to stand up for someone who needs assistance? Your core values are the driving force behind what you stand for, what is important enough to deserve sacrifice, and what it is that you would be willing to give up.

As a leader, you need to understand what you would and would not sacrifice for, as well as what you would be willing to sacrifice – pay, benefits, employment, well-being, etc. Be honest with yourself... if you falsely talk yourself into something being so important that you would be willing to sacrifice even if you aren't, you are setting yourself up for failure. In chess, if you are only willing to sacrifice pawns, you would be more careful in the movement of your other pieces, but your sacrifice is always done strategically. In your role as leader, those things for which you would sacrifice are also a matter of strategy, as determined by what is important to you and what you stand for.

Who do you serve?

Do you serve others or do they serve you? There can be no true self until you honestly determine whether you serve the interests of the organization or your own personal interests. Maria Drew, CEO and author, says it best, *"True leaders understand that leadership is not about them but about those they serve. It is not about exalting themselves*

but about lifting others up." If you are leading from the heart, you should find that by serving the interests of the organization you will also be serving your own interests. The key is to make sure you are not a self-servant leader and that you never allow your personal agenda to cloud your judgment regarding what is best for the organization and its members. **Remember, if serving others is below you, then leadership is beyond you** (anonymous quote).

> If serving others is below you, then leadership is beyond you.

Self-servant leader
 noun
Self-ser·vant | \ səlf ˈsər-vənt \
Definition of self-*servant leader*
: one that serves his or her own personal interest without regard to others
: one who believes others exist to serve the leader

What can you do?

Are you the best you can possibly be? Is there any personal growth possible or are you only as good as you were meant to be? These might seem like silly questions, but if you have a fixed mindset, then you will never be any better than you are now; your intelligence, skill level, talents, and abilities are all set, as they have been set

since you were born. You do not learn from failures, as they are simply the result of your limited abilities; you are uncomfortable with challenges, as they may lead to failure; you prefer to stick with the known, as the unknown may be beyond your abilities; you give up when frustrated, as you believe you either can do it or you can't; you dislike criticism, as there is nothing you can do to change your abilities. When an individual has a fixed mindset, there is a personal belief that there is no getting better, regardless of effort. A fixed mindset is sterile ground where the lack of learning, disdain for critical feedback, and fear of challenges inhibits personal growth.

Now, the opposite of that is the growth mindset. According to Carol Dweck, psychologist and seminal author on mindset, if you have a growth mindset, you view failure as an opportunity to learn (remember Chapter 5?), you embrace challenges as opportunities for

growth, you like to challenge yourself with the unknown, you welcome feedback as an avenue for self-improvement, and believe you can learn anything and get better at anything, as it is your effort, attitude, and persistence that will determine the outcomes. Unlike the fixed mindset, the growth mindset provides an individual with fertile soil for growth, as continuous learning provides the nutrients required for personal progress and development.

"The pessimist sees difficulty in every opportunity.

The optimist sees opportunity in every difficulty.

- Winston Churchill

Think about the Churchill quote you just read as you learn from the two shoe salesman:

> *Many years ago two salesmen were sent by a British shoe manufacturer to Africa to investigate and report back on market potential.*
>
> *The first salesman reported back, "There is no potential here - nobody wears shoes."*
>
> *The second salesman reported back, "There is massive potential here - nobody wears shoes."*

You can be an optimist or a pessimist, you can find barriers or opportunities, you can have a fixed or growth mindset. What can you do? That is entirely up to you. Anyone can have a growth mindset, just like anyone can have a fixed mindset. Your mindset is not something you are born with and stays with you your entire life. Much of your mindset is developed in your earlier years, based on your experiences and the lessons you learn from others, especially your parents and those you look up to. So, if anyone can develop a growth mindset, how does one find the path to a growth mindset? I believe in the path below, which is relatively simple to understand, involving 5 steps:

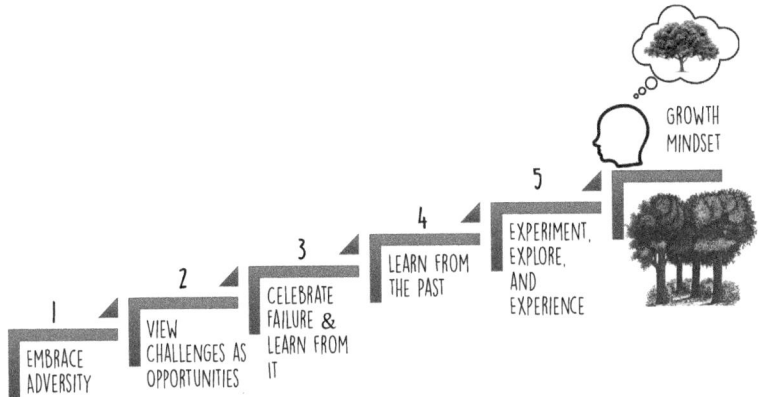

This staircase to a growth mindset is simple to understand, but it can be very difficult to train your mind for growth. First, do not fear adversity and do not try to avoid it... embrace it. Attack it head on, battle it the best way you know how, and if you come up short, realize that your efforts are not in vein and learn from your mistakes.

Along the same line of thinking, do not fear challenges. Every challenge brings the key to a new opportunity, all you have to do is open the door. Think about the parable of the old mule:

A parable is told of a farmer who owned an old mule. The mule fell into the farmer's well. The farmer heard the mule 'braying.' After carefully assessing the situation, the farmer felt sorry for the mule, but decided that neither the mule nor the well was worth saving. Instead, he called his neighbors together and told them what had happened and asked them to help haul dirt to bury the old mule in the well and put him out of his misery.

Initially, the old mule was hysterical! But as the farmer and his neighbors continued shoveling and the dirt hit his back, a thought struck him. It suddenly dawned on him that every time a shovel load of dirt landed on his back: he should shake it off and step up!

This is what the old mule did, blow after blow. "Shake it off and step up... shake it off and step up... shake it off and step up!" he repeated to encourage himself.

No matter how painful the blows, or distressing the situation seemed, the old mule fought "panic" and just kept right on shaking it off and stepping up. It wasn't long before the old mule, battered and exhausted, stepped triumphantly over the wall of that well! What seemed like it would bury him, actually end up blessing him.

– Author Unknown

The third step is taken when failure comes your way, as it certainly will along your journey. When it does, celebrate it as the greatest learning you could ever absorb. Remember what Churchill said, that failure is not fatal, and what Ford said, that failure is an opportunity to begin again more intelligently, and most importantly what Edison said, that there is no failure, just ways that things don't work. Weak leaders see every setback as a failure. Strong leaders see every failure as a mere setback. Your mindset will determine how you handle losses – they can make you stronger or cripple you, the choice is yours.

Next is what we do with the past. We all have choices to make – acknowledge our deficiencies, recognize our mistakes, own our failures, or ignore all those events that did not end with success, burying those memories of letdown so deep that there is not even a remnant of disappointment. One way leads to a better tomorrow while the other leads to greater heartache. Can you figure which is which? If we refuse to acknowledge our mistakes of the past and those actions or decisions that ended in disappointment, despair, or disaster, then it is

> Weak leaders see every setback as a failure. Strong leaders see every failure as a mere setback.

impossible to learn from them. It is true that you should not dwell in the failures of the past, but you must acknowledge them and recognize where you went wrong so that you can correct your errors and avoid the same discouraging outcomes in the future.

Finally, you cannot grow if you keep yourself constrained in your comfort zone. An individual who fails to push his or her supposed limits cannot grow, and is not a person worth following. You have to be willing to explore the world around you, even in those situations that make you uncomfortable. You must dare to experiment, trying new things, creatively solving problems, and exploiting or creating opportunities. Most of all, you must be willing to absorb the experiences, both good and bad, learning from all of them along the way. Every experience is an opportunity to learn and grow, and the more we explore beyond our comfort zone and experiment beyond that which we know, the more we will experience and the more we will grow.

Always keep Carolyn Dweck's words close to your heart, *"Love challenges, be intrigued by mistakes, enjoy effort, and keep on learning."*

Who controls your outcomes?

This is a critical question, and one that might surprise you if people honestly assessed themselves. This is a person's locus of control (LOC), which became an important psychological construct in the 1960s with the work of Julian Rotter. According to Rotter, an individual's locus of control is his or her belief system regarding who controls their outcomes, or their successes and failures. There are now widely accepted assumptions regarding LOC - there are two types of people – externals and internals.

An external, or person with an external locus of control, believes that their outcomes are out of their personal control, that external factors, chance, or powerful others control what happens to them. These are the people who make excuses – "It wasn't my fault," "It was bad luck," "It wasn't my time." When something bad happens, a "woe is me" attitude prevails. Externals generally give less effort and lack persistence, as they do not see the effort they exert having any significant influence over the results… it is out of their hands. If you are an external, you believe that others control your destiny; you have psychologically relinquished all power over what happens to you.

"Control your destiny or someone else will."

- Jack Welch

An internal, by contrast, has an internal locus of control, and believes that he or she controls their individual outcomes. These people believe the outcomes are the result of individual ability and the effort put forth, and not the result of luck or chance. Internals, due to their belief in the significance of effort, are likely to be more persistent when things are not going their way, and less likely to give up. Unlike the external's "woe is me," an internal's attitude is "I can do it." Internals believe they control their own destiny and maintain power over what happens to them. Whereas externals are excuse-makers, internals accept responsibility and learn and grow from each experience.

External

"I am a prisoner of the world around me."

Internal

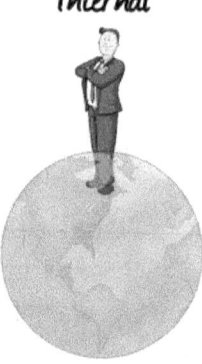

"I am in control of the world around me."

When you look in the mirror, you have to be honest with who you see looking back, and you have to be accepting of who you really are. By developing a growth mindset and employing an internal locus of control, you can always find a way to become a better person, but only if you are honest with yourself. The mirror provides a reflection, an exact version of your physical appearance, and so too must the mirror provide a true vision of your soul, who you are at the core.

"The only person you are destined to become, is the person you decide to be."

- Ralph Waldo Emerson

Be true to your values, improve on those characteristics you find detrimental, and work to be the best person and leader you can be… but always be authentic to who you are. President Abraham Lincoln warned all those who would come after him, ***"You can fool all of the people some of the time, and some of the people all of the*** *time, but you cannot fool all of the people all of the time."* I would add to that, *"… and you can never fool the man or woman in the mirror."*

Do not try to be someone you are not, for if you try to fool the people you lead, you will lose their trust, respect, and loyalty, and eventually you will find yourself a team of one.

Come to understand your values, develop a growth mindset, and harness an internal locus of control. Learn who you are and be true to that person; stand for what you believe and strive for what you desire. Above all, serve those who serve you.

WHO AM I?
SELF-ASSESSMENT

1. What is your finish line? What is it important for you to accomplish as a leader? What are your expectations of others? What drives you?

2. What are your core values?

3. What are you willing to stand up and sacrifice for?

4. Who do you serve? How do you serve those interests that are most important to you? Do you promote yourself or empower others?

5. How can you become a servant leader?

10 Build Bridges, Not Barriers

> "We build too many walls and not enough bridges."
>
> – Isaac Newton

Relationships are the key to successful leadership, both within the organization and with external partners. Whatever profession you call your own, forging relationships is going to be critical. Whether it is a nation's president building fellowships with members of the legislature and rapports with world leaders, or the principal of a school building relationships with staff, students, parents, and community leaders, successful leaders at all levels have to build bridges to others. I refer to the practice of building internal relationships as bonding, and external relationships as bridging.

Billy Crystal, famous comedian, said something very powerful when speaking of Muhammad Ali:

"Ali forced us to take a look at ourselves. This brash young man who thrilled us, angered us, confused and challenged us, ultimately became a silent messenger of peace who taught us that life is best when you build bridges between people, not walls."

Bridges connect people; barriers divide them. In this chapter, we are talking about relational bridges and barriers, not physical walls and bridges. This has nothing to do with the current immigration debate in the United States over Trump's wall, and whether or not it is a good or a bad thing. We are speaking of building the relationships that can help an organization grow and succeed, rather than ignoring those relationships at the risk of organizational failure.

Building bridges means we have to tear down barriers. Unfortunately, leaders often unwittingly construct barriers rather than build bridges. When a leader constructs barriers between leader and followers or allows barriers to develop between followers, he or she loses the ability to build bridges. At this point, the only way for bonding to occur is to break down the artificial barriers. So how and why do barriers arise within an organization?

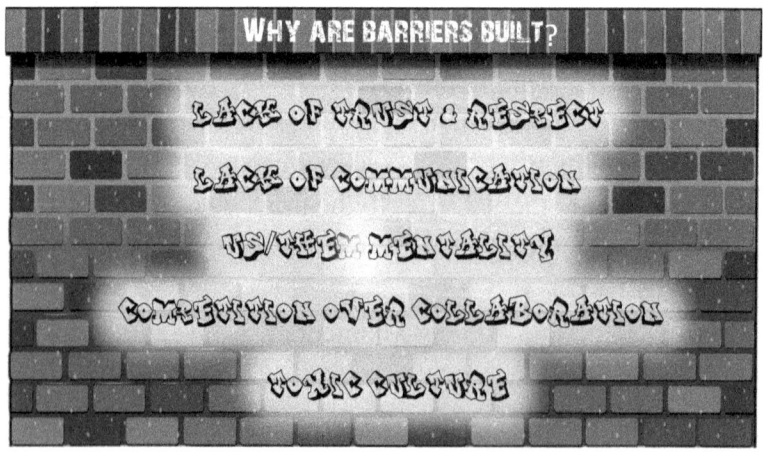

Lack of Trust and Respect

In *Be A Bean,* as well as throughout this book already, we have emphasized the importance of building relationships, and the necessity for there to be mutual trust and respect for these relationships to blossom. The lack of trust and respect is a double-edged sword – both sowing seeds and preventing growth. If the culture of an organization lacks trust and mutual respect, the culture prevents the growth of strong interpersonal relationships. However, it also spurs negative growth, and it does this by sowing the seeds of artificial barriers. These barriers will be erected between those individuals in the organization who do not trust and respect each other.

> The formation of artificial walls between individuals inhibits collaboration and community while fostering competition and isolation.

The formation of artificial walls between individuals inhibits collaboration and community while fostering competition and isolation. Man-made obstacles that prevent cooperation and promote separation actually transform commitment into compliance, leading to less productivity and negative organizational outcomes. The best way to avoid this fate is to work relentlessly to establish a culture of support where trust, respect, and loyalty permeate the organization. The path to breaking down already established barriers

> The path to breaking down already established barriers is to tirelessly toil to rebuild broken trust, deserve individual respect, and earn follower loyalty, while reforming the organizational culture to reflect those values.

is to tirelessly toil to rebuild broken trust, deserve individual respect, and earn follower loyalty, while reforming the organizational culture to reflect those values.

"There are no constraints on the human mind, no walls around the human spirit, no barriers to our progress except those we ourselves erect."
— Ronald Reagan

Lack of Communication

Another critical component of both developing strong relationships and preventing artificial personal barriers is communication. When there is a lack of communication, barriers naturally sprout. This gap in interpersonal communication fosters misunderstandings and further erodes existing trust. Poor communication is just as detrimental to organizational stability as the absence of communication. It is therefore necessary for members of the organization, beginning with the leader, to understand how to properly communicate. There are certain aspects of communication that minimize the possibility of miscommunication and increase goodwill between individuals. When communicating, individuals need to speak/write clearly and concisely, share with confidence, demonstrate empathy, and be active listeners. One should ask questions to understand what the other is saying without interrupting the purveyed stream of thought.

All communication should be conveyed on an equal footing, speaking or writing to the person as an equal of character, not speaking at the person as an inferior. Regardless of stature or position within the organization, everyone deserves to be communicated with as a human being and should never be made to feel like less of a person as a result of a conversation. With increasing amounts of ineffective communication, animosity grows, friendships suffer, teamwork dissipates, trust deteriorates, respect is lost, and walls rise. Effective communication, even when it is not what the individual wants to hear or read, is a valuable tool in earning the loyalty and respect of followers.

> With increasing amounts of ineffective communication, animosity grows, friendships suffer, teamwork dissipates, trust deteriorates, respect is lost, and walls rise.

Us vs. Them Mentality

When trust deteriorates or never exists in the first place, one of the most toxic aspects of a negative organizational culture can develop – the "us vs. them mentality." If it hasn't become obvious yet, trust is the key to construction – whether it is bridges or barriers being constructed, trust is the main component. Trust bonds, lack of trust divides.

> Trust bonds, lack of trust divides.

One of the main reasons for barrier construction is when a lack of trust produces divisions between leader and followers, between management and the employees, or between various divisions. This is often created by leaders who are dishonest, deceitful, and do not treat their employees with the respect they deserve. "Us vs. them" creates dysfunction within the organization, with different factions working toward their own goals amidst an atmosphere of distrust, isolation, and competition. When an organization endures the "us vs. them" mentality, collaboration is almost non-existent and support, whether sincere or not, is seen as a mechanism of micromanagement and control. When trust is so lacking as to foster such a divisive environment, any positive action is believed to have ulterior motives.

How do you overcome "us vs. them?" There is no easy answer and it requires a great deal of effort. Leaders must be willing to display vulnerability and find a way to bring dissenters back into the fold. This could require a meeting with representatives of the various factions in which everything is put on the table – each faction shares the reasons for their dissatisfaction and why they lack trust. The leader has to figure out how to help everyone realize how the organization's goals align with individual needs, and that by achieving the desired organizational outcomes, each individual employee will find personally desirable outcomes. There must be give and take where each faction is willing to give something to get something in return. The lack of trust makes this difficult, but this will be the beginning of a long, arduous process.

> "Us vs. them" creates dysfunction within the organization, with different factions working toward their own goals amidst an atmosphere of distrust, isolation, and competition.

Competition over Collaboration

Artificial barriers, by their nature, increase competition between co-workers and obstruct potential collaboration. When individuals lack trust and respect for one another, collaboration becomes extremely difficult. Colleagues who do not trust each other, cannot bring themselves to collaborate, and feel the need to compete regularly - for resources, for assignments, for the affection of leadership, etc. In a culture of competition, something positive for one employee is often perceived by others as bad for them. As a result, there is always the possibility of subversive efforts to ensure others do not get ahead.

Allowing employees to avoid collaboration only strengthens the barriers, erodes trust further, and strengthens the culture of competition. In order to break down barriers, leaders should increase the opportunities for collaboration, and these collaborative efforts must be significant, and the importance needs to be known by the collaborating employees. The importance of the task will ensure that these individuals will work together (as their jobs depend on it), forcing them to learn to trust each other, beginning the process of breaking down the barrier. Increased collaboration also reduces the probability of subversive action, as the employees are reliant on each other and if one fails, they all fail.

Toxic Culture

According to organizational culture researchers, Gruenert and Whitaker, *"The culture of any organization is shaped by the worst behavior the leader is willing to tolerate."* The more negative behaviors a leader allows, the more toxicity the culture develops. A toxic culture is a death sentence to any organization, as the negative perceptions and realities of such a culture weaken every part of the organization. So what is a toxic culture?

By definition, organizational culture is the set of shared values and beliefs... basically "how we do things around here." When culture is weak or negative, there is often a lack of these shared values, meaning individuals bring their own personal values into their decision-making and behavior. A toxic culture is a negative culture where trust is lacking, communication is poor, and major rifts permeate the organization. Members see leadership as adversaries, serving simply as judges, jury, and executioners, rather than as a support mechanism readily available to help members succeed. It is "us vs. them." Toxic cultures are driven by internal competition and foster an organizational climate where employees fear for job security, work out of compliance, and struggle to buy into leadership initiatives. Toxicity in a culture lowers workforce morale and job satisfaction, and perpetuates the construction of more barriers.

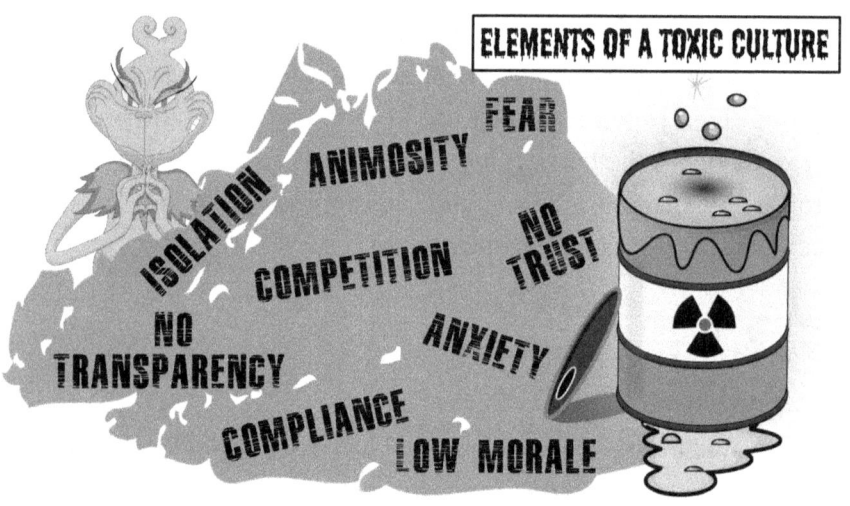

Niccolo Machiavelli famously said, ***"It is better to be feared than loved, if one cannot be both."*** I disagree. He also said that people are more willing to offend someone they love than someone they fear, which I have unfortunately found to be true. This is because love binds individuals in a way that fear never could. It strengthens the bonds of the interpersonal relationship, allowing people to feel the freedom to criticize, unlike fear which breaks bonds and stifles individual disagreement. As such, love fosters constructive conflict, whereas fear fosters destructive conflict. Fear also begets compliance, whereas love produces commitment. Commitment is a far more powerful motivator than compliance, and one that generally leads to better results.

Toxic cultures are cesspools of fear and compliance, and leaders who perpetuate or allow such an environment are not worthy of the title, leader. In *Be A Bean,* I advocated for leaders speaking not to the fears, but to the hopes of followers. In a toxic culture, where there is little respect, less trust, and no loyalty, the overwhelming combination of fear and animosity extinguishes hope. The love, of course, must come from strength - fairness, equality, respect, integrity, honesty, loyalty, transparency – not from pandering weakly to the whims of followers.

> In a toxic culture, where there is little respect, less trust, and no loyalty, the overwhelming combination of fear and animosity extinguishes hope.

If barriers are so damaging, why do leaders allow them to rise? Why would leaders want divisiveness, fear, compliance, stress, animosity, lower productivity, and all the other negative outcomes of the barriers existing in a toxic culture? Ignorance is one major reason, weakness is another, poor leadership, and finally... self-servant leadership. Many leaders do not know any better and are totally oblivious to the negative roots growing within

> Self-servant leaders thrive on dysfunction, dividing staff so that they cannot unite in opposition, creating an ethos of fear and anxiety so individuals comply without dissent, and flouting transparency to shroud the truth of their hidden agendas and personal interests.

their organization. Others are simply to weak to garner the control and demand the respect required to prevent barrier construction. Still others are simply poor leaders, lacking the knowledge, attributes, and skills to develop a positive culture. Self-servant leaders, however, are different. They are usually cunning, knowing full well of the seeds they sow. They are weak in that they fear relinquishing control, but hold power over followers, using fear to control the masses. They thrive on dysfunction, dividing staff so that they cannot unite in opposition, creating an ethos of fear and anxiety so individuals comply without dissent, and flouting transparency to shroud the truth of their hidden agendas and personal interests.

Building Bridges

For those leaders who serve the interests of the organization, it is always possible to break down barriers and build bridges. There is no secret formula to building bridges, but there are some helpful hints that will go a long way toward making those bridges a reality. Before getting into the things that help us build bridges, let's take a look at a parable demonstrating the power of building bridges rather than barriers.

The Parable of the Two Brothers

Once upon a time there were two brothers who were the best of friends. Born just a couple years apart, they grew up doing everything together, side by side. Side by side, they explored the hills and the streams and the woods that surrounded their parents' farm.

Side by side, they ate breakfast in the morning. Side by side, they brushed their teeth before bed at night.

They played sports, did their homework, helped with chores, played pranks on their parents—and they did it all side by side. The neighbors said, "Those two boys are joined at the hip." That was the neighbors' way of saying that the brothers couldn't be separated. And the neighbors were right.

After high school, the brothers decided they wanted to be farmers like their parents. They saved up their money and they bought two farms, and those farms were—you guessed it—side by side. The farms were in a beautiful valley. They had lots of grass where the horses and cows could graze. And it had rich, healthy soil where good crops could grow. There was even a pretty little creek that ran between the two farms. For years the brothers farmed next to each other. They helped each other. They shared tools and machines. They shared some of the food that they grew.

Many nights during the summer and early fall, after a hard day's work, the two brothers would meet at the creek to talk and swim and fish and watch the sun set over the valley. They did this side by side too. And the neighbors said, "Those two brothers are thick as hair on a dog." Which was another way of saying that the brothers couldn't be separated. But this time the neighbors were wrong.

The brothers got into a quarrel. It was their first serious fight ever. It started out as a little misunderstanding, but it grew into a big argument. The older brother was certain that the whole thing was the younger brother's fault. The younger brother was just as certain that the whole thing was the older brother's fault. They started yelling, and they said hurtful things to each other. Then they stopped talking altogether. The longer the silence, the angrier both brothers got. They stopped helping each other. They stopped sharing tools. They didn't go near the creek where they used to meet to talk and fish. Days went by. Then weeks. And it seemed like the two brothers who had always been the best of friends would never be friends again.

Then one morning, when the younger brother was finishing his breakfast and grumbling crossly to himself, there was a knock on his door. When he opened it he found a man carrying a toolbox. The man said, "I am a carpenter. I'm in the area for a few days, and I'm looking for work. Do you have any small jobs I can help you with?" The younger brother had a flash of inspiration. "As a matter of fact, I do," he said. He pointed across the creek. "Do you see that farm? That farm belongs to my older brother. We're quarreling and it's all his fault and I'm furious at him. I want you to use the pile of lumber by my barn to build a fence along the creek. I want it to be eight-feet high. No twenty-feet high! I don't want to see his property—or his face—ever again!"

The carpenter thought for a moment. Then the carpenter said, "I think I understand the situation. I'll be able to do a job that pleases you."

The younger brother had to go into town for the whole day. But before he left he helped the carpenter get the materials ready. Down to the side of the creek they hauled lumber, nails and screws, and tools of all kinds. The younger brother took one last look at his brother's farm, then left to run his errands. As the younger brother's car disappeared from sight, the carpenter got busy. He worked hard. As he measured, sawed, and nailed, he thought a lot about the two brothers. The day was hot, but the carpenter was skilled and he did a fine job.

Just as the sun was setting over the valley, the carpenter finished his project. He was loading his tools into the truck when the younger brother returned home. The younger brother was eager to see the fence he had asked for. But when he got out of his car, his jaw dropped. He couldn't believe his eyes. There was no fence there at all.

Instead, there was a bridge.

It was a simple bridge but it was sturdy and, he had to admit, lovely to look at. It stretched from one side of the creek to the other.

But the bridge wasn't even what surprised him most. What surprised him most was the sight of his older brother coming across the bridge, his arms outstretched. The older brother said, "What a wonderful brother you are to build this bridge! Thank you!"

The brothers met in the middle of the bridge. First, they shook hands awkwardly. Then they got down to business and hugged each other and apologized to one another for all the hurtful things they had said and done. When the brothers turned to thank the carpenter, they saw he was hoisting his last toolbox into the back of his truck. "No, wait!" said the younger brother. "Stay a few more days. I have a lot of other projects for you."

The carpenter smiled and wiped his brow with a handkerchief. "I'd love to stay on," he said, "but I have to go. I have many more bridges to build."

As the brothers watched the carpenter drive away, they promised that the next time they had an argument they would meet in the middle of that bridge and work it out. They would stand there and work it out—side by side.

The Parable of the Two Brothers demonstrates how easy it is to erect barriers, even for those who are as close as the two loving brothers. It also shows how important it is to build bridges and bring people together. What happened that built the barriers between the two brothers? Each brother felt the other brother had disrespected him, each brother developed a negative attitude toward the other, they closed off their minds to anything positive from or about the other brother, they no longer supported one another, and they lost their personal connection as time went by. The bridge changed all that, opening their minds, reminding each of their love for the other, reviving that special personal connection.

This is how a leader builds an environment in which bridges can be built – treating everyone with respect and being fair and equitable, conveying a positive attitude with an open mind, supporting all, and making personal connections with each and every individual in the organization. One more thing about the parable... a leader is like the carpenter, constantly on the move and "having more bridges to build."

The Planks of an Effective Bridge

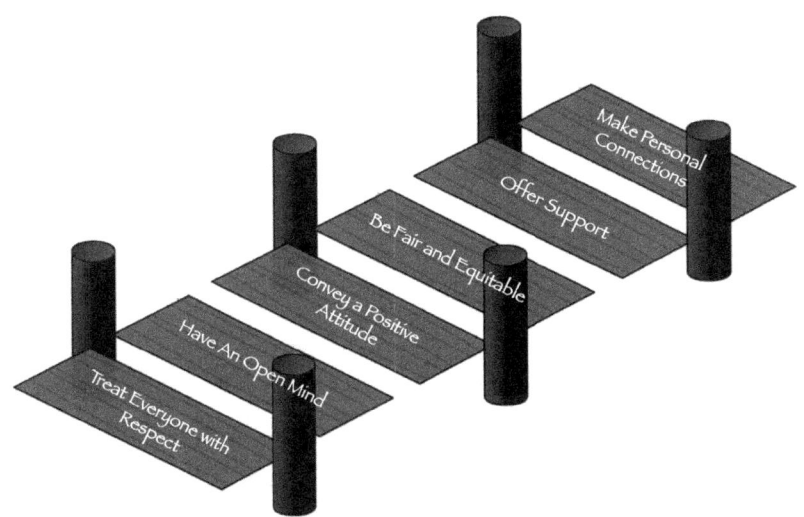

Treat Everyone with Respect

The foundation of building bridges is respect, for without respect there is less trust, and without trust, as we have seen, nothing good happens. A wise leader stresses respect for others with every decision he or she makes and every action he or she takes. Treating others with respect requires that a leader communicates with an individual or group on equal footing, despite rank. This doesn't mean equality in authority for the two, but it means that the leader respects the individual enough to speak to him or her, not at him or her. In other words, leaders do not talk down to others, or flaunt their authority. It also means that the leader clearly participates in two-way conversation, listening actively as well as speaking. It's important that followers know that the leader truly listens to what they have to say. Another requirement is that the leader makes fair and equitable decisions, not showing favoritism, ensuring that each individual in the organization has equal access to resources, and equal opportunities for promotion, bonuses, supplemental positions, stipends, etc.

Have An Open Mind

A closed mind erects barriers. An open mind can build bridges. When a leader operates with an open mind, he or she invites questions, accepts criticism, and respects alternative opinions. Such a leader endears him or herself to others, earning the trust and respect needed to develop strong interpersonal relationships. By understanding that you do not know everything, you do not have all the answers, and your ideas are not always going to be the best, you afford your followers opportunities to be heard, to contribute to the organization, and to fulfill their personal actualization needs. An open mind contributes greatly to employee empowerment and perceived ownership in the outcomes of the organization. What better way to bond with followers then to listen to their opinions, value their contributions, and empower them to make a difference?

Convey a Positive Attitude

A closed mind erects barriers. An open mind can build bridges. In the same way, attitude often determines which construction begins. Leaders with positive attitudes generally engender more trust and respect from followers, opening the door to bridges, whereas a negative attitude lays the bricks for barriers. Positive attitudes open up a lane for communication and sharing of ideas, optimism and empowerment, whereas a negative attitude stifles such opportunities as individuals prefer to avoid contact and keep to themselves.

Be Fair and Equitable

It is impossible for a leader to bond with others if he or she is seen as unfair and biased. If you want to build strong relationships with your followers so that they commit to you and your cause, it is necessary for them to see you as fair and equitable in your decision-making. Promotions should be obtained only through excellent work and/or superior ability. Raises should be earned based on job performance. Everyone should have equal access to the leader, and all members of the organization should be treated with the same respect, and all individuals should have the same opportunity for advancement. Without these things, there will be compliance rather than commitment. Once there is perceived favoritism, it will be extremely difficult for the leader to earn the trust and respect of those not perceived as favored, and barriers rather than bridges will be built.

Offer Support

This is simple enough. "How Can I Help?" If you remember back in Chapter 2, we said it was a leader's responsibility to help in any way possible. If a leader is seen as readily available to help a follower, one who can be counted on as a steady source of support, a bridge is already being built. Offering support for those outside of the organization is also a way to build bridges with external partners. Support, however, must be genuine, and assist the individual in completion of the task, not merely a gesture to generate the appearance of support.

Make Personal Connections

If interpersonal relationships are as critical as I have been saying, and trust and respect are the keys to earning loyalty and commitment, then the formation of personal connections is at the top of the leader's "To do" list. Establishing personal connections with followers allows the leader into their personal world, the follower's inner sanctum. It allows the leader to build empathy, gaining him or her more credibility in conversations with the individual. The greater the personal connections between leader and follower, the greater the trust, respect, loyalty, and commitment will be. Personal connections mean establishing a relationship beyond the workplace, not physically, but mentally. These connections generate greater understanding between those involved, and a greater desire to maintain good relations and a strong association, greatly enhancing the leader's influence. It is very easy to ask how an employee's sick grandfather is doing, but it makes a world of difference as to how the leader is perceived. Be aware of what is going on in your followers' lives, and do not be afraid to share personal conversation when appropriate.

Break Bridges but Don't Burn Them

Nothing is ever going to be perfect and there will be times when relationships take hits. If enough time and effort was put into developing them, and the relationships are strong, built on mutual trust and respect, then they will be able to absorb the hits and continue on. During tough times, when there are problems between leader and follower or between various followers, if it becomes necessary to alter the relationship, how you deal with it can determine whether or not the relationship can be repaired. If the rift is large enough, break the bridge, but don't burn it. In other words, take some time off from the relationship, avoid confrontations with the individual, deal with him or her a little bit differently until the time and circumstances are right to heal the relationship. By only breaking the bridge, you can repair it, no matter how much it was damaged and how difficult it might be.

However, if you burn the bridge, if the rift is so bad that individuals said horrible things to each other, intentionally hurt one another, or in any way tried to undermine the other's position within the organization, there is no going back. The relationship would have to be built from scratch, which is usually not amenable to either side. Breaking is temporary, it happens often, and can usually be repaired. Burning is permanent and usually is irreparable.

Don't Be Afraid to Make Enemies

Although a leader should always prefer to avoid burning bridges, there are some bridges that should be destroyed forever. There is no need to have bridges, and to waste any time and effort bonding to those who are immoral, unethical, subversive, and who actively work against the mission and vision of the organization. However, there are good people with whom a leader may find a crumbling bridge, whether by disagreement over policy, personal friction, competitive desires, or any other of a number of sources of tension. In these instances, it is often a better idea to mend the fence, or build a bridge where one never existed. Abraham Lincoln, who you will read about later, and a man who had more enemies than a simple man could imagine, thought, *"I destroy my enemies when I make them my friends."* Following the teaching of Lincoln, building bridges can eliminate enemies and save a leader much dissension and heartache, and possibly even create powerful allies.

In the end, however, a true leader must never fear making enemies. Enemies are those individuals who disagree with, speak out against, vilify, and try to undermine, for the purposes of advancing a different agenda. Enemies does not have to mean a personal hatred exists, or that one wishes harm on another, but simply people with differing agendas, opinions, or ideas that are in stark contrast to one another.

The only leaders that go through life without having made enemies are those who were too timid to make a difference. A leader who is willing to take a stand, speak out against injustice, promote a needed policy with unpopular appeal… these are leaders who will make enemies. They are also leaders who will make a difference. Any time a person takes a stand, or firmly supports one position in opposition to others, he or she will make enemies. It is simply how humans work. Some of the biggest difference makers in history had plenty of enemies. Let's look at one…

> A leader who is willing to take a stand, speak out against injustice, promote a needed policy with unpopular appeal… these are leaders who will make enemies. They are also leaders who will make a difference.

Abraham Lincoln, the 16th President of the United States, was elected in 1860 at the height of the slavery debate in the nation.

His election spurred the Civil War, with the southern states attempting to secede from the union, and Lincoln doing everything within his power, and perhaps even beyond his constitutional power, to maintain the union. He was vilified by loyal southern confederates, slave owners, and secessionists because of his strong and often questionable actions taken in the hopes of abolishing slavery and maintaining the union, but even in the North, his base of power, there was great vitriol and serious doubts. Even within his own Republican party, he was far from popular. His suspension of the writ of habeas corpus, the law that prevents American citizens from unjust imprisonment, in 1862, and declaration of martial law in 1863 led many to label Lincoln a tyrant, claiming he was usurping the authority of Congress and unconstitutionally expanding his executive powers. Lincoln presented the Emancipation Proclamation to the nation in 1862, leading the Chicago Times to declare it, "a monstrous usurpation, a criminal wrong, and an act of national suicide." He pushed for the passage of the 13th Amendment to the U.S. Constitution, outlawing slavery, for which he often found himself making questionable deals to earn support from members of Congress.

Regularly referred to as a dictator and tyrant, Lincoln never wavered from his decisions once he had made them. Although he made enemies with every decision, every action, every speech, and every policy, Lincoln never shied from journeying down the road less traveled, always his own man, never afraid to take a stand or find himself embroiled in controversy, and never concerning himself with his growing list of enemies. To no one's surprise, the president suffered from depression and often existed in a state of melancholy, but he always did what he thought was right and stood by his decisions, regardless of the enemies they made him. In the end, Lincoln was assassinated, his life ending early, shortly after his reelection as President of the United States. His life was over, but his legacy lives on today… a nation of 50 united states, free of the scourge of slavery, where all men and women are equal under the law.

"You have enemies? Good. That means you've stood up for something, sometime in your life."
- Winston Churchill

    If you are serious about being an effective leader and guiding your organization to growth and success, then you will have to make tough decisions, and most decisions will not be unanimously supported. You have to be okay with disappointing people, offending people, and upsetting people, because you will not be able to make everyone happy. Remember, everyone has their own personal agendas and individual desires and needs. Leaders can only worry about those so much as they impact the advancement of the organization's goals. If you are the kind of person who needs approval, who needs to be everyone's friend, or who needs to to have unconditional support, then you are not, and can never become a true leader. There will be those who disapprove of your decisions, those who find your actions unnecessary or unwise, and even those who will violently disagree with you in public. You must be able to find peace with the fact that you will have opposition, that many of these individuals will become your enemies.

Put forth the effort to develop strong relationships, build trust, and earn the respect and loyalty of your followers so that your organizational culture values bridge building and bonding while breaking down barriers.

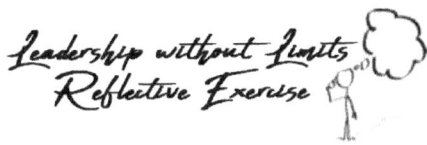

BRIDGE BUILDER OR BRICKLAYER?

1. How many of the elements of a toxic culture does your organization share? Would you classify your culture as positive or negative? Why? What about climate… how do members of the organization perceive the environment in which they work?

2. Based on this chapter, how many bridge builders do you have in your organization? Are you a bridge builder?

3. What kind of barriers exist in your organization?

4. How can you remove the barriers in your organization and build bridges?

5. Have you made enemies? If so, why? How did you react to this opposition? Did it offend you?

11 Follow the Road Less Traveled

"Do not follow where the path may lead. Go, instead, where there is no path and leave a trail."

Ralph Waldo Emerson

Earlier, I advised you to be a nonconformist, to think differently, act differently, defy conventional wisdom, and challenge the status quo. Much in the same breath, I ask you not to follow the path of convention, the path that is safe and offers little resistance, for that path also offers little achievement. Why follow a path taken by so many before you? To become one of many, to do what everyone else has done, to accomplish what has been accomplished many times before? To travel this path is to travel a path with many footprints, so many that no one will ever be able to tell which are yours. In others words, you will leave no discernable footprints behind, your legacy will be that of everyone else and nothing more. If, however, you choose to follow the path of the road less traveled, if you dare to go where others have failed to go, if you are willing to brave the unknown, risk failure, and blaze your own trail, then there is much for you to accomplish. And the footprints… the world will know they are yours! Yours can be a legacy of great accomplishment and awe-inspiring contributions to the development of a kinder, safer, more peaceful world.

What footprints will you leave behind?

Katie Couric says, *"Be fearless. Have the courage to take risks. Go where there are no guarantees. Get out of your comfort zone even if it means being uncomfortable. The road less traveled is sometimes fraught with barricades, bumps, and uncharted terrain. But it is on that road where your character is truly tested. And have the courage to accept that you're not perfect, nothing is and no one is — and that's OK."* The road less traveled can be less safe and more daunting, and will probably challenge you beyond what you could have expected on the path of least resistance, but the reward will be tremendous if you can harness the fear, handle the discomfort, and persist through the gauntlet of obstacles. All the challenges of the road less traveled are temporary, as is any pain associated with your travels along it. The achievement, however, will last forever, as will the spirit of triumph that grew from your journey.

Barack Obama, 44th President of the United States, says, *"If you're walking down the right path and are willing to keep walking, eventually you'll make progress."* Which is the right path? How do we know? Successful businessman Adam Draper tells us to *"Pave your own path and be fearless."* That is the right path! That is the path to travel, and to continue to travel to make progress… not the path that has been paved before, but the path that you discovered. Einstein agrees, declaring, *"The person who follows the crowd will usually go no further than the crowd. The person who walks alone is likely to find himself in places no one has ever seen before."*

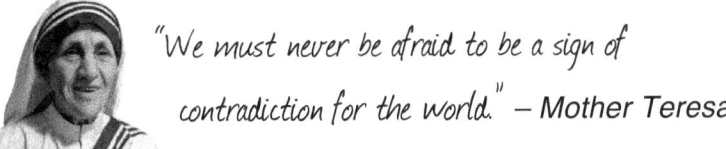

"We must never be afraid to be a sign of contradiction for the world." – Mother Teresa

Greatness lies in achieving what you determine you can, what you determine is important, and what you determine to be your proper course in life. **The road less traveled is not a physical place, but a mental one. It represents nonconformity, independence, and individuality. The road less traveled is a metaphor for you being you, making your own decisions, and choosing your own path.** At times, this may very well be the more popular path, but this is a decision that you need to make, based on your experiences, your knowledge, your goals, and your abilities, and not a decision made because everyone else is doing it.

Following the path of others, living by their decisions, journeying toward their chosen destination, relying on the past experiences of others, and conforming to what society expects or wants, these are the road more traveled. This path does not lead to new destinations, but to previously explored ends. There is little to no discovery along this path, meaning little to no achievement. It also means making little difference for your organization, in the lives of others, or in the community.

Perhaps this is your desire… to leave a legacy of non-existence, to refrain from leaving discernable footprints, and to simply be an obedient follower to society's norms and expectations. Perhaps you have no desire to challenge your limits and find out how special you can be or how much you can achieve if you dare to be different. Perhaps you are nothing more than a sheep, maintaining your place within the herd. If this is you, then join others on the journey to the known. Take the simple path rather than daring to challenge yourself.

If, however, you wish to leave a legacy, if you wish for your footprint to be big and bold, if you want to make a difference, do not be afraid to step upon that road less traveled. Do not be afraid to determine your own destination, make your own choices, think and act differently, endure criticism and naysayers, and if need be, stand alone. Taking the road less traveled often involves going against convention, swimming upstream so to speak, against the current of popular opinion. Those who make a difference are not afraid to buck society and do their own thing. Winston Churchill, one of the frequent flyers on the road less traveled, likened it to flying a kite, *"Kites rise high against the wind, not with it."*

Your road less traveled may not be the same as others, and your path could be similar or different from others. The important thing is that it is your path, the desired destination of your choosing, that the journey is littered with the people you have selected to join you and the choices you have made to give your expedition direction, and that you have prepared yourself for every bend, twist, and turn that you will most certainly encounter along the way.

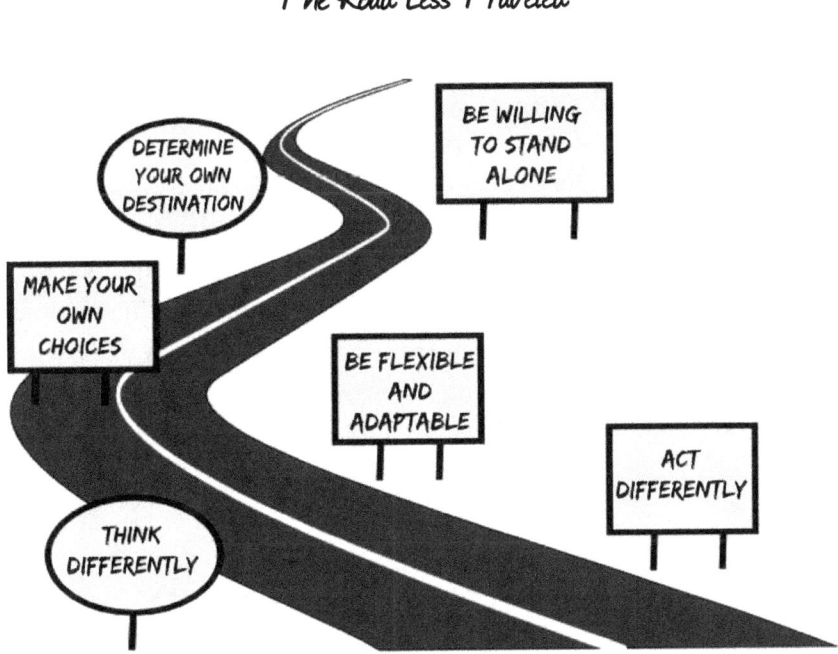

The Road Less Traveled

Throughout your life, others will try to pressure you to fit in, to be like everyone else, and travel the path that others before you have chosen, but your destiny should not be of another's making. You shouldn't worry about being normal and fitting in… just ask Maya Angelou, who suggests that *"If you are always trying to be normal, you will never know how amazing you can be."* You were born to be you, born to travel the path of your choosing, born to impact the world in the way that only you can. Be special, be amazing, follow the road less traveled and make a difference!

> *"If a man does not keep pace with his companions, perhaps it is because he hears a different drummer. Let him step to the music which he hears, however measured or far away."* – Henry David Thoreau

Robert Frost told us, *"I – I took the road less traveled by, and that has made all the difference."* What did he mean by it? That is for the reader of his poetry to determine. For me, the road less traveled is everything we have so far seen in this chapter, with one addition. Often, when we journey the road less traveled, we find ourselves doing things that have never done before – delicious new recipes, new technologies, new services, new treatments, curing illness, and so many other things that improve our quality of life, extend the average life expectancy, and make life easier and more productive.

Things Not Done Before
by Edgar A. Guest

The things that haven't been done before,
Those are the things to try;
Columbus dreamed of an unknown shore
At the rim of the far-flung sky,
And his heart was bold and his faith was strong
As he ventured in dangers new,
And he paid no heed to the jeering throng
Or the fears of the doubting crew.

The many will follow the beaten track
With guideposts on the way,
They live and have lived for ages back
With a chart for every day.
Someone has told them it's safe to go
On the road he has traveled o'er,
And all that they ever strive to know
Are the things that were known before.

A few strike out, without map or chart,
Where never a man has been,
From the beaten paths they draw apart
To see what no man has seen.
There are deeds they hunger alone to do;
Though battered and bruised and sore,
They blaze the path for the many,
Who do nothing not done before.

The things that haven't been done before
Are the tasks worth while to-day;
Are you one of the flock that follows,
Or are you one that shall lead the way?
Are you one of the timid souls that quail
At the jeers of a doubting crew,
Or dare you, whether you win or fail,
Strike out for a goal that's new.

The road less traveled, as we have described it thus far, is being different, doing your own thing, making your own choices, determining your own destination, and not taking the path of least resistance or that path which is popular and safe, but striking out on your own and leaving your own mark. But... what about thinking? Does the way one think influence his or her path? ABSOLUTELY! Those who think like the pack, will act like the pack, and follow the path of the pack. Those who think differently, will act differently, and discover their own path. The parable of the babies and the river teaches readers the importance of thinking differently and traveling your own path:

> Those who think like the pack, will act like the pack, and follow the path of the pack. Those who think differently, will act differently, and discover their own path.

> *A group of people are standing at a river bank and suddenly hear the cries of a baby.*

> *Shocked, they see an infant floating and drowning in the water.*

> *One person immediately dives in to rescue the child.*

> *But as this is going on, yet another baby comes floating down the river, and then another!*

> *People continue to jump in to save the babies and then see that one person has started to walk away from the group still on shore.*

> *Accusingly they shout, "Where are you going?"*

152

He responded: "I'm going upstream to stop whoever's throwing babies into the river."

Lesson: We cannot solve problems by thinking the same as everyone else and by doing things the same way everyone else has. The road less traveled offers opportunities and solutions that just can't be found continuing down the same old trodden path. In the parable above, the crowd was simply addressing the result of the problem – the drowning babies – but it took the man thinking differently, choosing his own different path, to deal with the cause of the problem – the people throwing the babies into the river. The road less traveled led to solving the problem, not just dealing with the results. When you are sick, do you want to deal with the symptoms or get rid of the infection that has caused the symptoms?

Remember, the road less traveled doesn't always have to take you to far off places, earth-shattering events, or momentous, life-altering actions. The road less traveled can simply take you somewhere you haven't been, somewhere you didn't expect to go, doing something you never dreamt of doing, or maybe just in a different direction than others. It is your road, and the travel is yours, that is the important thing. As long as you are making your own decisions, you are deciding where to go, and you are being true to your own self, thinking and acting as you see fit, not as the world expects or wants, then you will find yourself on the road less traveled… and hopefully find your destination as grand as you dreamed.

When life brings you to a crossroads, and you have the choice to follow the herd or venture on the road less traveled, have the courage to go where others haven't been and discover your own path.

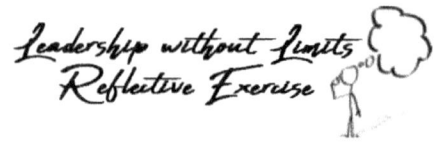

ON WHICH ROAD DO I TRAVEL?

TRUE or FALSE:

1. I prefer to stick to things I have already done and know how to do.

2. I would usually choose to do something safe for which I know the outcome, rather than risk failing at something new that has potential for greater reward.

3. If everyone I am with decides on a path, I will naturally just go along with them.

4. I am a conformist.

5. I am a conventional thinker.

6. I do not like to risk embarrassment by sharing ideas and opinions that are different from what has already been heard.

(False answers lead to the road less traveled.)

OPEN-ENDED:

1. Have you ever journeyed the road less traveled? Describe any instances, and explain how this would be considered the road less traveled.

2. Think of an instance in the near future when you might have the choice between which path to take… how can you take the road less traveled and make a positive difference in another's life, your organization, or the community?

12 Evolution or Extinction?

"The greatest danger in times of turbulence is not the turbulence – it is to act with yesterday's logic."

— *Peter Drucker*

The world is constantly changing, and with it so are the markets in which our organizations exist and the professions in which we find ourselves. If we continue to move forward in the exact same way we did the day before, not only will we find ourselves not making progress, but we will actually find ourselves falling further and further behind the competition. As the world turns and the markets shift, so too must our leadership evolve, thinking and acting not for yesterday, not even for today, but for tomorrow. As legendary Hall of Fame basketball coach, Mike Krzyzewski says, ***"Leadership is an ever-evolving position."***

Merriam-Webster has many definitions of evolution, with a couple pertaining to the type of progression we are discussing in this chapter. The first definition is "a process of change in a certain direction." The other is, "a process of gradual and relatively peaceful social, political, and economic advance." When we speak of leader evolution, we are talking about a leader who thinks differently as circumstances change, who proactively engages change rather than reacting to the results of it, and who is flexible and adaptable enough to identify or create, and exploit, opportunities as external and internal environments change. The leader's principles and core values will never change, although his or her words, actions, and behaviors by nature, must.

> When we speak of leader evolution, we are talking about a leader who thinks differently as circumstances change, who proactively engages change rather than reacting to the results of it, and who is flexible and adaptable enough to identify or create, and exploit, opportunities as external and internal environments change.

"Change your opinions, keep to your principles; change your leaves, keep intact your roots."
– Victor Hugo

The current world is an amalgamation of chaos, change, ambiguity, and complexity that offers both tremendous promise and potential disaster at every turn. A leader must have the intellectual agility, meaning he or she must be flexible and adaptable, to effectively evolve with the ever-changing landscapes of the postmodern condition. A flexible leader is one who has the ability to effectively change his or her thinking, alter tactics and strategies, and shift resources in response to a potential or current change in the external or internal environment. One who is adaptable has the ability to consistently, continuously, and successfully navigate the organization through varying environments. Together, flexibility

> A flexible leader is one who has the ability to effectively change his or her thinking, alter tactics and strategies, and shift resources in response to a potential or current change in the external or internal environment.

and adaptability make a leader agile. Leader agility is something my mentor, Dr. Pisapia, stressed as critical to successful leadership in the 21st Century, sharing this slide representing the importance of a leader having many actions available to him or her:

The Evolution of Leader Actions

In the past modern age with slow moving change and stable markets, leaders with a specialized set of skills, and a limited set of actions available was sufficient for organizational success. In this postmodern condition, with rapid change, chaos, complexity, and ambiguity, leaders must evolve. Like an artist has many colors on the palette from which to choose, a leader now must have many actions on the leadership palette from which to choose. The more agile a leader, the larger the palette, and the more actions available to him or her.

What does this all mean?

Using basketball as an example:

On one hand, a flexible coach would be one who is an effective in-game tactician, one who can change defenses on the spur of the moment to counter an opponent's changing offensive strategy, can effectively make substitutions to negate potential advantages gained by the opponent changing personnel, and can successfully utilize timeouts to halt opponent surges.

An adaptable coach, on the other hand, would be one who could coach teams with differing personnel, managing a small, quick pressing team just as effectively as a tall, strong, slower, half court team. A coach who is adaptable would also be able to game plan equally effectively against a press defense as a half court defense, or a team that runs motion offense as a team that runs set plays.

Pat Riley is an example of an "agile" leader, demonstrating the flexibility and adaptability required to evolve. His masterful strategizing and in-game coaching (flexibility) have combined with the adaptability of being able to coach differing sets of personnel with different styles with the LA Lakers, New York Knicks, and Miami

Heat. The result… five NBA championships as a head coach and two more as an executive.

Using teaching as an example:

A flexible teacher is one who can proactively engage potential problems or effectively react to unforeseen incidents during a lesson, or effectively pivot from one strategy to another to more effectively communicate content that is not being understood by the students, basically making on-the-fly changes to the lesson plan to deal with the changing environment of the classroom.

An adaptable teacher is one who can teach various subjects, diverse student populations, or equally well using various pedagogical methods. Such a teacher can serve vast populations and in multiple capacities due to his or her ability to be consistently effective despite diverse learning abilities and differing educational needs.

These are just two examples of what I mean by flexible and adaptable. They are not all-inclusive; for example, there may be other ways in which a teacher can demonstrate adaptability, but hopefully these examples help you to understand the difference and connection between the two. Basically, while both involve a leader's ability to deal with environmental changes and stressors, flexibility is short term and adaptability is long term. To successfully evolve, a leader must be both flexible and adaptable, or in other words, agile.

Although we have been focused on the leader, the organization, itself, must also be made to be flexible and adaptable. The best ways to accomplish an "agile" organization is to make sure it is "fit," not just a fit for the market in which it exists. Remember, evolution is "survival of the fittest!"

Components of a "Fit" Organization:
1. Little Bureaucracy
2. Smaller divisions with limited independence
3. Distributed leadership with autonomy

A fit organization is one that is "lean," meaning that there is very little bureaucracy to slow down decision-making and stymie the organization's ability to take action. The only positions that exist are those that are necessary to the functioning of the organization and critical to the fulfillment of the mission and vision. Along with reducing bureaucracy, an organization can be made more agile by constructing it in a way that there are smaller divisions with limited independence to make decisions, proactively seek out and exploit opportunities, and react to potential problems without having to include other sectors of the organization not directly involved. This means autonomy for leaders throughout the organization in a distributed leadership structure. With leadership distributed throughout various parts of the organization, it can more quickly react to changes in the environment and competitors in the market, and be more proactive in seeking out opportunities.

An organization with centralized leadership, inflated bureaucracies, and a convoluted departmental structure are "out of shape" and cannot effectively react to environmental changes with enough speed to evolve. Often due to a lack of trust, insecurity of the leader, or constant mismanagement by abdication or micromanagement, these organizations are incapable of making timely decisions and taking necessary actions. They generally lack the flexibility and adaptability to successfully navigate the ever-changing minefields of the current postmodern condition, and will struggle to maintain their position in the market.

What happens if leaders and organizations fail to evolve?

Does anyone remember the dinosaurs? I mean, of course, what happened to the dinosaurs. I am sure we all know that they went extinct, that they no longer exist. Whether it was because of an extinction level event or a failure to adapt to changing environmental conditions, we no longer have dinosaurs roaming our planet today. A leader who is unable to evolve because he or she lacks the agility to do so will find that there is no longer a leadership position available. An organization that fails to evolve will find itself out of the marketplace and facing its own demise. The choice for a leader is simple... evolve or face extinction.

The father of evolutionary theory, Charles Darwin, proposed his theory of natural selection as the mechanism by which species evolve. Put simply, this means that those organisms that were best adapted to the environment in which they existed would survive and reproduce, while those that failed to adapt would die off, eventually giving rise to a new species. This is no different in leadership, as those who are more flexible and better adapted to the changing landscape in which their organizations operate, are likely to find success and create sustainable organizations, while those who lack such abilities will find it difficult to continue.

A leader who fails to adapt to the changing landscape in which the organization currently exists, or one who is inflexible to the point of failing to make quick course corrections or change his or her thinking to fit the shifting environmental conditions, will find that the organization can no longer survive with his or her leadership and must make changes to avoid its own irrelevance. It does not matter how intelligent a leader is, or how skilled he or she is in dealing with people, if the leader is not flexible enough to adapt to changing environmental conditions. The leader who will survive and prosper is the one that is agile, flexible and adaptable enough to evolve with environmental changes and guide the organization down the constantly shifting path of the postmodern marketplace. Those who are not agile will find that they have lost the ability to lead, that the organization requires new leadership, and they will find their final place amongst the dinosaurs… extinct!

> The leader who will survive and prosper is the one that is agile, flexible and adaptable enough to evolve with environmental changes and guide the organization down the constantly shifting path of the postmodern marketplace.

Leaders today must be flexible and adaptable, capable of diverse thinking and a wide array of actions, demonstrating the agility to evolve with changes in environmental conditions and the ability to navigate an organization through chaos, complexity, ambiguity, and change.

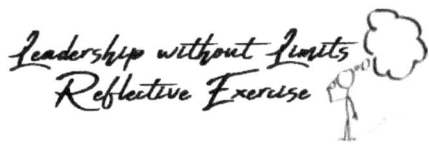

Can I Evolve?

1. What skills do you have that would allow you to succeed in diverse environmental settings?

2. Are there particular settings in which you are more comfortable and others in which you are uncomfortable? Explain.

3. Do you prefer to lead a certain population of followers or are you comfortable around all different types of people? Explain.

4. Can you change your thinking in response to changing environmental conditions? If so, provide and example and explain. If not, how can you learn to do so?

Dr. Keith G. Feit

13 Fett's Final Limitless Advice

I'd like to leave you with some advice that I believe could help you along your leadership journey. Hopefully, the words contained in these chapters inspired you in some way to challenge the limits of your leadership and always ask why not.

1. It is better to be loved than feared.

Always remember that commitment is a far more powerful motivator than compliance. Love produces commitment while fear generates compliance. Followers' love for a leader grows parallel to increasing levels of trust, mutual respect, and demonstrated loyalty, and is fostered by an environment of fairness, equity, honesty, and support. Build those strong interpersonal relationships throughout your organization, and promote such relationships amongst all members.

2. Admit your mistakes and guide course corrections.

We are all human and we all make mistakes. Admitting your mistakes, learning from them, and correcting them is a sure way to earn the trust and respect of your followers. Denying responsibility for mistakes and projecting blame onto others are the path to a toxic culture in which there is little to no trust, respect, or loyalty, and compliance far outweighs commitment.

3. Speak to the hopes of others.

As a leader, you will always have the choice as to whether to motivate by hope or fear. Try to consistently carry with you a positive attitude and an optimistic outlook, and speak with the goal of inspiring your followers. Inspiration is more likely to gain commitment, while fear, as said earlier, generates compliance.

4. Encourage, promote, support, and model entrepreneurial spirit.

Creativity, curiosity, questioning, experimentation, and innovation are all extremely important attributes leading to success in the 21st century. For the members of your organization to feel comfortable taking risks, being proactive, and pursuing innovation, you, as the leader, must model these attributes yourself, encourage them amongst your followers, promote opportunities for them to engage in such a manner, and provide support for both successes and failures. If there are negative repercussions from leadership resulting from employee entrepreneurial intentions and behaviors, then the entrepreneurial spirit of members, as well as the organization as a whole, will be extinguished.

5. Be bold, be different, and never be satisfied.

It is easy to be cautious, to promote an incremental approach to change, and to encourage such behaviors in your followers. At times, this is even necessary, but when it comes to the overall essence of your organization, throw caution to the wind. Dream big and dare big!

The safest path is to be like everyone else, but that is not where achievement lies. That is not where greatness lies. If you think and behave like everyone else, you will follow their path. To think differently, to act in unconventional ways, these lead to your own distinct path, one which will allow you to make a difference.

Satisfaction is the assassin of progress. To be content means there will be little desire to change, to attempt to improve, to dream bigger. Remember what Thomas Edison said, that for there to be progress there must first be discontent. Never be satisfied with where you have been, where you are now, or where you are going. Always aim higher, dream bigger, and dare greater... always attempt to be greater than you ever thought possible.

6. Celebrate failure as a bridge to success.

If you have never failed, then you have never tried to accomplish anything of value. We all fail, we all come up short. Promote within your organization an attitude that failure is nothing more than a temporary setback and a necessity for the learning that will lead to eventual success. Be sure to look at failures as setbacks, rather than setbacks as failures. When one comes up short, it is but a bump in the road, not the end of the journey. Failure is an obstacle to be overcome, not a barrier at which to quit.

7. Always be authentic, transparent, and honest.

To be an effective leader, you must be true to who you are, never trying to be someone you are not. Be real, show your followers the true you, not some stranger hiding behind a mask. Authenticity is easy to spot, and inauthenticity is even easier. If you fail to demonstrate authenticity to your followers, then you will never develop the trust and respect necessary to support strong interpersonal relationships, and your organization will become a den of compliance. Always be transparent and honest in all your dealings with members of your organization, even in moments of disagreement and discord. A bond built on false pretenses will not last, and will most likely lead to a harsher separation than if truth and transparency were the original intent.

8. "C" your way to success...

The path to success involves effective leadership, which comes from efficacious use of the 6 C's... Clear, concise, consistent, communicative, critical, and collaborative. An effective leader must be clear in terms of goals, values, aspirations, expectations, standards, processes, procedures, and the like. He or she must be concise, keeping things as simple as possible for followers to understand, and consistent in terms of enforcement of organizational policies and procedures and fairness, especially the equitable treatment of employees. A leader must be communicative, always keeping followers "in the loop," providing updates, sharing advice, offering support, and informing them when performance requires improvement, all while being critical, maintaining high standards, ensuring all members are living up to the standards that have been set, and all members are effectively working towards the organizational mission. This involves another "C," constructive criticism, which is necessary for followers to learn and improve. Finally, an effective leader is collaborative, understanding that all members are part of a team, that nothing is achieved in isolation, and that the best outcomes are usually produced from a combination of the skills, talents, opinions, ideas, and suggestions of various individuals.

9. DARE!

Dare to dream.
Dare to be bold.
Dare to defy convention.
Dare to challenge.
Dare to question.
Dare to disrupt.
Dare to be creative.
Dare to be different.

Dare to master chaos.
Dare to be your best when things are at their worst.
Dare to speak up.
Dare to be you.
Dare to make a difference.
Dare to change the world.

10. Enjoy the Journey!

Leadership, like life, is a journey. Don't be so focused on the destination that you forget to enjoy all that you experience along the journey – laughs and tears, relationships built and relationships lost, successes and failures, overcome challenges and missed opportunities – for these experiences have the potential to make you a better leader and a better person.

Finally, always ask why not...

Be the leader who seeks reasons to try rather than reasons not to.

Be the leader who focuses on the potential upside, rather than the possible downside.

Be the leader who sees opportunity, not dead ends.

Be the leader who emphasizes that things can get better, as opposed to the one that stresses how bad things are now.

Be the leader who welcomes adversity, rather than hiding from challenges.

Be the leader who emphasizes what you can become, not what you are.

Be the leader that finds a way to how instead of the leader who finds a way to "no."

ABOUT THE AUTHOR

Dr. Feit is an educator, author, and researcher with a Ph.D. in educational leadership. Throughout a life involving many leadership positions at varying levels within organizations, including committee chairman, team leader, department leader, board chairman, and commissioner, Dr. Feit has gained vast experience and achieved success as a leader. His books are a collection of his philosophies, thoughts, ideas, strategies, and inspiration to be shared with all.

Be sure to read all the books in the Feit Leadership Series:

Be A Bean!
Life Lessons for Anyone and Everyone Who Wants to Live a Good Life, Be a Better Leader, and Change the World

Anyone Can Be A Bean:
Ordinary Individuals Who Became Extraordinary People

Don't Ask Why:
Leading Without Limits

Little Bag of Beans:
Quotes, Parables, Poems, Fables, & Tales
to Inspire Your Journey